THE VIRTUES

THE
VIRTUES

JOHN H. GARVEY

THE CATHOLIC UNIVERSITY
OF AMERICA PRESS
WASHINGTON, D.C.

Printed in Canada

The paper used in this publication meets the minimum
requirements of American National Standards for
Information Science—Permanence of Paper for Printed
Library Materials, ANSI z39.48-1984.

∞

Cataloging-in-Publication Data available from the
Library of Congress

ISBN 9780813236223

CONTENTS

CONTENTS

THE VIRTUES

INTRODUCTION

T HE NOVELIST Tom Wolfe famously preferred exploring the unfamiliar. His third novel, *I am Charlotte Simmons*, looks at the culture of America's elite colleges and universities. It considers what sort of people graduates of these institutions are likely to be when they step out into the world. Charlotte Simmons, a young woman from rural North Carolina, is his subject. The story follows her as she adapts to life at the fictional Dupont University. Wolfe's argument is that there is a crisis in our elite universities. They are bigger, wealthier, and more beautiful than ever. But they are failing to do what we built them for.

Charlotte arrives at Dupont University as a promising student but by the middle of her first semester her grades are terrible. She's lost track of her principles. She's unhappy and lonely. She's become untethered from her moral upbringing and sense of who she is. From her very first moment at Dupont her rural Christian upbringing is out of place. Faced with a choice to adapt to the new moral environment or remain lonely and alienated, Charlotte chooses to adapt. She embraces the moral code of her peers. At the end of the novel, as she ponders the ways she has changed in a semester and a half, she recalls her mother's warning: "There's gon' be folks here wanting you to do thangs you don't hold with ... And if anybody don't like that, you don't have to explain a thang to'm. All you got to say is, 'I'm Charlotte Simmons, and I don't hold with thangs like 'at.'" She wonders what her mother would say if she could see her now. And what about her soul? Does she even believe in a soul anymore?

The novel poses a provocative question. Is Charlotte's choice to adapt really a free one? Can goodness thrive in a moral wasteland? Is it likely to? Charlotte thinks she is free. Wolfe isn't so sure. One thing is certain: Charlotte is not a better version of herself for having attended Dupont University. That's a sign of decay Wolfe wants us to notice. In some ways things are as they always were at elite institutions. Graduates still receive competitive degrees; they still learn from world-class faculty; they get jobs in finance and go to the best law schools. But a critical piece of their education is missing. They aren't learning how to live well. In fact, many have learned how to live badly. New York Times columnist David Brooks wrote of *I am Charlotte Simmons* that "[Wolfe has] located one of the paradoxes of the age. Highly educated young people are tutored, taught and monitored in all aspects of their lives, except the most important, which is character building... they find themselves in a world of unprecedented ambiguity ... where it's not clear if anything can be said to be absolutely true."[1] Everyone agrees that colleges and universities are responsible for teaching students calculus and French literature and the laws of thermodynamics. But are they responsible for teaching them to make good judgments, or to be courageous? Is moral education the job of a university? Brooks thinks the answer is yes. So do I.

This book reflects on the university's role in the moral education of its students and on what it might look like to do that well. Wolfe's Dupont University certainly provided Charlotte Simmons a moral education of a kind. By the end of the novel, some of the most important people on campus think she's cool. Dupont's basketball coach knows her by name; uni-

1. David Brooks "Moral Suicide a la Wolfe" (NYT, November 16, 2004)

versity administrators speak about her in hushed whispers. She's revered by the same sorority sisters who mocked her virginity and called her a "tumor" only months before. In a weird way, she is a success. She has become like them. But she's better at it than they are.

There is a kind of excellence in all of this but it's the wrong kind. It looks a little like virtue but it lacks goodness. Charlotte fits in, and it feels good. But no one would mistake what Charlotte has for real happiness. That's what makes the novel a tragedy. Charlotte has conquered campus but lost herself. She has conformed to its ideas about how to live exceptionally well and forfeited her own. Of the senior who got her drunk to take advantage of her in her first semester, she now says "He hadn't betrayed her at all. Hoyt was what he was, the same way a cougar was a fast animal that stalked slower animals, and that was what a cougar was." College was supposed to give Charlotte a better life. It was supposed to help her to become a better version of herself. Wolfe's title, *I am Charlotte Simmons*, is intended ironically. Dupont University has not made her a better version of Charlotte Simmons. By the end, it has erased her.

The setting of *I am Charlotte Simmons* is a fictional place. We can't be sure of what it might have said about moral formation. But it likely would have had a mission statement that sounded like those of other elite institutions. Harvard's says this: "The mission of Harvard College is to educate the citizens and citizen-leaders for our society" through the transformative power of education.

Beginning in the classroom with exposure to new ideas, new ways of understanding, and new ways of knowing, students embark on a journey of intellectual transformation.... From this we hope that students will begin to fashion their lives by gaining a sense of what they want to do with their gifts and talents, assessing their values and interests, and learning how they can best serve the world.[2]

Compare this to one adopted at an earlier stage of Harvard's history. Shortly after its founding in 1636, Harvard replaced its original motto (Veritas) with another: In Christi gloriam ("for the glory of Christ"). A third came in the late eighteenth century: Christo

2. Harvard University "Mission, Vision, and History." Available at https://college.harvard.edu/about/mission-vision-history

et Ecclesiae ("for Christ and Church"). The historian Samuel Eliot Morison writes that

In Christi gloriam ... expressed the fundamental object of [its founders] .... Like the medieval schoolmen, they believed that all knowledge without Christ was vain. Veritas to them, as to Dante, meant the divine truth ... The first college laws declared that every student was to be plainly instructed that the "maine end of his life and his studies" was "to know God and Iesus Christ ... and therefore to lay Christ in the bottome, as the only foundation of all sound knowledge and Learning."

The religious identity of places like Harvard once maintained the connection between their intellectual and moral purposes. The intellectual purpose was knowing God; the moral purpose was serving God. Today God is harder to find at Harvard. So is the connection between the intellectual life and the moral life. Students are exhorted to gain "a sense of what they want to do with their talents and gifts" through exposure to new ideas. But it's up to them to figure out who they want to be and how that connects to their studies.

You might take from this discussion that places

like Harvard strive to be morally neutral. There may even be official messaging to that effect. But I don't think it's true. Like all universities, Harvard has moral priorities and strives to pass them on to its students. What has changed since the days of Christo et Ecclesiae are the content and means of its moral education. The content is less clear; the means less obvious. But that doesn't mean its moral influence has lost significance. Let me mention a few of the ways moral influence plays out in universities.

Here's an obvious one: Universities make decisions about which intellectual pursuits are important (and which are not). For some universities the purpose of an education is connected to wisdom. They think a student shouldn't graduate without reading Shakespeare or Plato so they require their students to take courses in literature and philosophy. Some focus exclusively on the great books. Other universities swing in the opposite direction. Their primary aim is to prepare students for a profession. Studying classical texts might be an option, but it is not necessary. There are fewer core classes at these universities; instead, the focus is on advanced courses in an area of specialization. The universities I have taught at have tended to emphasize both. In each case the intellectual aims put forward reflect a moral purpose. A university that emphasizes liberal arts education does so because it thinks it is good for students to know the liberal arts. One that emphasizes advanced engineering instead also has a moral purpose.

Here's another, from my own experience: Universities make lots of decisions about how to shape life on campus for undergraduates. Many of them have moral significance. In 2011 The Catholic University of America, where I am president, opted to go against a trend and return to single sex dorms. At the time I cited studies that show the ill effects of co-ed housing on student behavior. Binge drinking and hooking up are more common in co-ed dorms.[3] There is evidence that having multiple sexual partners leads to higher rates of depression in young women. Sexually active young men tend to perform worse academically.

Our aim was to avoid these ill effects. It was also to encourage students to forge healthier, deeper relationships, and to foster thoughtfulness about the con-

3. Wall Street Journal "Why We're Going Back to Single-Sex Dorms." June 13, 2011. Available at https://www.wsj.com/articles/SB10001 42 4052702 30443230457636984 3592242356

nection between sex and commitment. Over the past several decades, many colleges and universities have moved in the opposite direction. Some have even introduced co-ed rooms. Often the rationale is that it honors student preferences and gives students the opportunity to learn to interact with the opposite sex. This encourages students to take a more experimental approach to sex. These policies take a different view of sex and commitment than we do. But they are no less morally significant.

Here's one more example. If you visit Alabama during football season or UNC during basketball season, there is no mistaking the important role college sports play on campus. This is another way universities exert a moral influence. In 2017 Clemson spent over $46 million on its football program. Duke spent nearly $21 million the same year on basketball.[4] Competitive athletic programs are not a bad thing. They're often a good thing. Athletic competition gives student athletes a chance to develop and show their excellence. It can be inspiring for their classmates. College

4. James G. Martin Center for Academic Renewal "Mirror, Mirror on the Wall, Who Spends the Most on Athletics of All?" September 23, 2019. Available at https://www.jamesgmartin.center/2019/09/mirror-mirror-on-the-wall-who-spends-the-most-on-athletics-of-all/

sports can build camaraderie and bring people back to campus after they graduate. But there are also downsides. Prioritizing sports on campus can come at the expense of other endeavors—sometimes the most important ones, like academics or the practice of faith. It can also raise moral questions. Sometimes it can lead to a hero-like status among athletes. It can lead to corruption in administrations.

The point is this: students will take a moral lesson from what their university chooses to honor. If the starting point guard is treated like royalty by a university administration, students will learn to treat him like royalty too. If a college invests heavily in its physics or music program, students are more likely to view those areas as important. If it spends millions on a new library collection, students will take note of that too. The reverse is also true. If a university underfunds its philosophy or literature programs, students will likely see these as less important. If the only space to worship on campus is the dining hall basement, that will tell them something too.

More rarely, colleges and universities take an official position on a particular moral issue. Our students at Catholic University march on the anniversary of *Roe v. Wade* each year at the March for Life in Washington, D.C. I join them because my university believes unborn babies have a right to life and we want our students to share in that commitment. In the 1990s I worked at the University of Notre Dame. There is a famous photo of Fr. Ted Hesburgh, who was university president at the time, walking arm-in-arm with Martin Luther King. The university prominently displayed it in the 90s as it does still today. The photo is important to the university because it shows its commitment to racial justice. It keeps it on display because it wants to impart that commitment to its students.

It's not just religious colleges that make these moral gestures. In recent years colleges and universities have expanded their efforts to make their campuses more diverse and inclusive. Last year Columbia University offered six separate graduations, dividing students based on income level, race, and ethnicity.[5] A college in California did something similar and offered a Lavender (LGBTQIA+) graduation. In both

5. National Review Online "Columbia University's Ultra Woke Idea." March 23, 2021 Available at https://www.nationalreview.com/2021/03/columbia-universitys-ultra-woke-idea-segregated-graduation-ceremonies/

cases the institution in question wanted to impart a final moral lesson to its students about how it thinks we ought to approach difference.

Here's my point. Education has changed since Harvard declared its motto to be Christo et Ecclesiae and John Witherspoon lectured on the connection between liberal education and moral virtue at Princeton. A few colleges and universities continue to perceive a connection between the intellectual life and the moral life. Many believe they have become neutral spaces. On closer inspection, however, it becomes clear that these universities have a moral program. They aim to inculcate certain moral values in their students. If Tom Wolfe is correct, they do so with a measure of success. The question isn't whether colleges and universities are offering moral education, but what sort of moral education they ought to impart.

Mozart is famous for his operas, and *Don Giovanni* is arguably the best among them. One reason for that is the brilliance of its main character. A seducer, Don Giovanni charms women through deception, uses them for pleasure, and then discards them. The famous catalogue aria numbers his exploits in the thousands. His sins get even worse than this. Early in the opera he attempts to assault Donna Anna, and when he's caught, he kills her father in a duel. He's habitually cruel, even to his faithful sidekick, Leporello; he respects no one, not even the spirit who comes to take his life. At the conclusion of the second act, just before he meets his fate, he repeats the line "io mi voglio diverter" ("I want to be amused"). The words nicely sum up his character. They also suggest one way to think about freedom.

The question of the kind of moral formation we ought to offer our students is connected to how we understand freedom. Don Giovanni represents a libertine approach. Desire is foremost. Freedom is the absence of obstacles to getting what he wants. This is an extreme view. But it has something in common with a more popular understanding. In *Planned Parenthood v. Casey*, an abortion rights case from the 90s, Justice Kennedy offered a view of freedom that stems from a similar idea. He said, "At the heart of liberty is the right to define one's own concept of existence, of meaning, of the universe, and of the mystery of human life." Freedom is about maximizing your ability to define your own existence. It is the ability to choose your own adventure, or to "live your truth."

Catholics tend to look at freedom differently. Saint John Paul II said that freedom is "not the power of doing what we like, but the right of being able to do what we ought." This kind of freedom takes goodness, rather than choice, as its reference point. It is about conforming ourselves to what God made us to be, not about maximizing our options. Wordsworth offers a similar idea of freedom in "Nuns fret not at their Convent's narrow room" when he says

> *Hermits are contented with their Cells;*
> *And Students with their pensive Citadels;*
> *Maids at the Wheel, the Weaver at his Loom,*
> *Sit blithe and happy ....*

His point, and St. John Paul's, is that freedom should be directed toward an appropriate end. You or I might find the constraints of a convent or a hermit's cell difficult. But to a sister or hermit at prayer, these are places of freedom. The hermit's cell minimizes his choices but makes it easier to do what he ought. That's why "In truth the prison, into which we doom/ Ourselves, no prison is." Something similar is true of a maid at the wheel and the weaver at his loom. Their tasks do not constrain them; they give them direction. In that sense they make them more free, not less. In Wordsworth's case the constraints of the sonnet liberate his poetry.

> [A]nd hence for me,
> In sundry moods, 'twas pastime to be bound
> Within the Sonnet's scanty plot of ground;
> Pleased if some Souls (for such there needs must be)
> Who have felt the weight of too much liberty,
> Should find brief solace there, as I have found.

The virtues are habits that channel our freedom in the direction we ought to go. They are principles of action that move us to do good things. "Only virtuous people are capable of freedom," Ben Franklin says. That's not what Casey says (freedom is the right to define your own existence) or what Don Giovanni practices. For Franklin, as for John Paul II, freedom is not a license to do as you please. It is the ability to move easily and without hindrance in the direction of what is good.

This is still fairly abstract. What is it about virtue that channels our actions in the right direction? And what exactly will we find if we travel that direction—toward what Wordsworth calls that "narrow room" where we can "[s]it blithe and happy?"

~

Let me begin with the channeling power of virtue. Today we often think of habits in a negative way, as forces that exert an unwelcome influence over our choices, like a smoking habit or a late-night eating habit. On this view habits oppose what we truly desire—a healthy lifestyle, for example. But the idea of a habit once had a richer meaning. Habits were linked to freedom rather than opposed to it. Aristotle thought that habits formed a kind of 'second nature' that allows us to do what is good easily, even instinctually. He thought that we acquired this second nature through practice. Over time our repeated good actions form stable qualities in our souls.

It sounds simple, but it's not. Situations that require our moral attention are often complicated. It can be difficult to judge what is best to do, especially when the different paths we might choose each yield an obvious benefit. Even when we can see what the best choice is, there can be obstacles to desiring it. Sometimes we would prefer a different outcome.

Sometimes the better choice will make us uncomfortable. It might be easier to have a cigarette at the end of a long day. Choosing to eat a slice of cake in the middle of the night might be comforting. And there are other ways a choice to act well can be complicated. Choosing what is good may not serve our immediate interests. It may even cost a job promotion or a friendship. We know from the stories of saints and heroes that choosing what is good sometimes demands more dramatic sacrifices than these. It may even require sacrificing one's life. Finally, even in cases where the desire is present, it can be difficult to follow through on the choice.

St. Augustine would say that all of our moral choices—even bad ones—are directed toward obtaining something good. Making a moral choice involves choosing the highest or most appropriate good in a situation. But we are drawn to lesser goods all the time. Cake is good. So is the pleasure we have in eating it. But in the middle of the night, after you have already had a piece or two, another piece of cake may not be a healthy or moderate choice.

This is where moral habits come into play. They help inform both our knowing and our acting. The more we do good acts, the more easily we recognize what we ought to do in other circumstances. We also find that we can do those things more easily. It's not unlike physical training. Think about the first time you tried to play basketball. Unless you are Kobe Bryant, your jump shot was probably pretty lame. But if you spent five or six years practicing, you almost certainly developed a better shot. At some point you built up and coordinated the right muscles. You began to understand what a good jump shot feels like. Eventually, taking a jump shot seemed natural.

Moral habits are similar. They develop through practice. At first it is difficult to forego a second piece of cake, or to stick to one beer, or to go to bed on time, even when we plainly see that these are what is best for us. But over time moderation becomes easier. The obstacles that stand in the way are still there, but we are more successful in surmounting them. Our success derives from the moral habit we have developed. Eventually, like a good jump shot, choosing moderation becomes easy to do. In fact, we do it without a second thought. It becomes an integral part of our game.

Something else happens, too. Over time we are

able to adapt the habit to more difficult circumstances. It's hard to think about temperance in heroic terms. Usually we don't face a firing squad when we choose to forego a second piece of cake. But there are moments when temperance requires a little heroism, like when your friends are urging you to drink too much, or when your Italian grandmother puts another cannoli on your plate.

Like muscles, moral habits become stronger the more we use them. But unlike muscles, moral habits become a part of who we are. Building muscle changes how I look and what I can do. But in itself it doesn't change my character. Building moral habits does. Over time my moral habits change who I am. With repetition, the choice to stick to one beer, forego a second piece of cake, or go to bed on time shapes my soul. Moderation is not only something I practice, it is something I am. That's why Aristotle calls it a habit, or a "having." Over time I come to possess these moral qualities as a part of myself.

Moral theologian William Mattison describes habits as "a sort of middle ground between a person and the person's acts." Though they arise from repeated action, habits are more permanent than actions. A bad basketball player can occasionally make a good shot. But we don't call him a good player on that account. The reverse is true too: a good basketball player can make some bad shots. But he is not a bad player for that reason. The difference between a good and a bad basketball player does not rest in single actions, good or bad, but in stable habits. A good player has perfected a good shooting technique. He has developed the muscles and the form to execute a good shot. He also has a sense of when to shoot and when to pass. All of these skills require practice.

Something similar is true of our moral character. A person of poor character can act well at times. Walter White commits all kinds of atrocities throughout the TV series *Breaking Bad*. In the end, he attempts to rescue Jesse from imprisonment for apparently benevolent reasons. It is a noble enough action, but it doesn't make him virtuous. Likewise, a good person can fail to act well at times. Think of King David. But good habits make this less common precisely because they create a disposition in the one who has them. Good habits make doing the wrong thing unnatural to us, and doing the right thing natural.

And what is the point of developing these practices? They will form us into a particular kind of person, but why is that the model we should aspire to? Perhaps Justice Kennedy was right. Perhaps we should define our "own concept of existence, of meaning, of the universe."

Aristotle proposed another way of approaching the issue. He said that in deciding how we ought to live, we should begin by asking what makes us happy. Happiness is unique among human goods because it's something we desire for its own sake. All other goods provide temporary satisfaction or joy, but only happiness brings us complete fulfillment. When we examine our desire for other things with a critical eye, we see that the reason we want them, ultimately, is that they will make us happy.

The kind of happiness Aristotle has in mind is not a feeling. Feelings are important, but fleeting. They aren't a reliable indicator of what will give us satisfaction in the long run. Happiness in the deep sense is more like a completion or fulfillment of purpose.

Stanley Hauerwas says that Jane Austen is one of history's great moral teachers. Perhaps as well as anyone else, she understood that human happiness should serve as the basis for morality. Maybe that's why I like her novels so much. Every few years someone attempts a movie adaptation of one of them. About a third of the time, their efforts are successful. A new version of *Emma* was released last year. Whit Stillman directed an adaptation of *Lady Susan* a few years before that. Kiera Knightly starred in an adaptation of *Pride and Prejudice* in 2005. Every director seems to get that the love story is important. But only the good ones understand the connection between the love story and virtue, and if you miss that, you miss everything.

The virtues connect goodness with happiness. Think about *Pride and Prejudice*. After being slighted by Mr. Darcy, Elizabeth couldn't imagine him capable of kindness or generosity, much less love. In failing to allow the possibility, she revealed her own lack of kindness and generosity of opinion. Mr. Darcy's pride, in turn, blinded him to Elizabeth's and Jane's virtues. His declaration of Elizabeth's unworthiness revealed his own. Both Elizabeth and Darcy were unfit to marry at the beginning of the novel. The manifest virtues each one had were obscured by vices, by pride and prejudice. Only after correcting those vices were they made fit for one another. The happiness of their marriage was a consequence of their growth in goodness. The well known BBC film adaptation understood this; the 2005 adaptation missed it.

Pride and Prejudice is probably the most famous example, but the connection between marriage and virtue is on center stage in all of Austen's novels. Marianne Dashwood lacks temperance and patience to tame her passion. Emma Woodhouse is prideful, imprudent, and vain. Catherine Moreland needs to learn courage and wisdom. In each case the central character must first grow in virtue; romantic love follows after. Novels about romance are generally about the incompleteness of two people. We perceive them as unable to live without one another. Austen's novels say the opposite. They are about people who perfect aspects of their own character and, as a result of that, they are able to see and admire one another better. The real drama happens when each character grows in prudence, wisdom, or generosity. The romance is just the finale.

Another of Austen's novels highlights the last point. It's less popular than *Pride and Prejudice* and *Sense and Sensibility*, and for good reason. The story moves slowly. It has fewer fireworks. Its heroine, Anne Elliot, is less vivacious than Elizabeth Bennett or Marianne Dashwood. She is sensible and cautious (to a fault). She lives seven years in regret, having lost Frederick Wentworth, the man she loved, to her own lack of courage. Her story, like those of the other Austen heroines, ends happily. She marries Wentworth and we are happy for her. But she doesn't deliver the youthful passion we get in *Emma* or *Sense and Sensibility*. Hers is a story of mature love.

Persuasion makes the point the other novels do about the connection between virtue and a good marriage. But it offers something else too. The young Anne Elliot's downfall resulted from a lack of courage in her convictions. Her struggle speaks in a particular way to the importance of virtue in higher education. Living virtuously requires a special kind of courage. Anne Elliot didn't trust in her own virtues and succumbed to social pressure. This is similar to the temptation many young people face today. Even those who have good intentions can easily be persuaded to do something vicious. *I am Charlotte Simmons* makes that point too. I suggested at the beginning of this introduction that the virtues deserve a special place in university life. Anne Elliot and Charlotte Simmons illustrate several reasons for that. Let me mention a few others.

The purpose of the university is to educate. When students arrive on campus we exhort them to make the most of their years here. We provide them opportunities to learn about almost any conceivable subject. We provide academic services to guide them on the path of learning. Our buildings are designed to remind them of this purpose. All of these external aids exist to help fulfill the purpose of the university, the education of young minds.

But they are only aids. As every successful student knows, the real work of education takes place in the soul. World class scholars offer instruction in the arts and sciences. Academic advising provides information and even some guidance. But deciding what and how to study takes prudence and wisdom. Resident Assistants can preach about how to balance school work and social life, but all the advice in the world will not make up for a lack of temperance. Even the beauty of Gothic architecture and its reminders of the towering intellectual achievements of the West are only an invitation. A good student needs to cultivate a love of knowledge and the perseverance to pursue it.

The point is that university life only works alongside the cultivation of virtue. The intellectual life depends on the moral life. Without virtue we cannot sustain the practices necessary for advanced learning. In fact, without virtue, it's hard to see what the purpose of the university is. Learning begins with love (for the truth). If we don't have that, it's hard to know why we would bother with education at all.

But there's much more to it than that. What a student learns in the classroom will follow her into life. But a university education is not limited to fifteen credit hours a week. Undergraduates who begin college as teenagers graduate four years later with adult responsibilities. A marketing major might soon after be a mother. A philosophy student will have the responsibilities of a citizen. A future senator might study political science, but the prudence he practices now will shape his public service. Universities have an obligation to prepare students for these roles, too.

❧

In many ways, I have been writing this book for the past 20 years. Since my time as a law school dean at Boston College I have chosen some particular virtue as the topic of my commencement remarks. I have continued that practice at Catholic University. For much of my time here I have also taught a course entitled The Virtues to freshmen in the Honors Program. Those materials form the foundation for this book.

As I noted at the beginning of this introduction, this book is not a philosophical or theological examination of the virtues. It draws occasionally from the wisdom of philosophy and theology as well as from literature and culture, but what you will find here is more reflective than analytical. My observations are things I might say to one of our grandchildren who was about to embark on a university education. My aim is not to provide information but to stimulate thinking. In the following pages I will examine a number of virtues in practice, considering what wiser people than I have had to say about them, and how virtuous people have lived them.

The book is divided into several large sections, each consisting of several chapters apiece. Each large section collects a different group of virtues. The first is about the theological virtues, faith, hope, and charity; the second, the cardinal virtues of justice, temperance, fortitude, and prudence. The third section focuses on what I have called (borrowing from St. Francis de Sales) the "little" virtues. The last considers wisdom, peace, and joy, the crown of the virtues. In keeping with a more reflective tone, the chapters are brief and conversational. My aim is to have each do what a good conversation does: invite deeper thinking about something of importance. I hope you will find some wisdom there as well.

THE THEOLOGICAL VIRTUES

I DON'T THINK MUCH OF Woody Allen's movies. I think even less of his philosophy. But sometimes he writes good characters. Occasionally he captures a way of looking at the world better than anyone else. There's a certain worldview that looks for redemption without a redeemer. Allen captured it with this line from *Crimes and Misdemeanors*: "It is only we, with our capacity to love, that give meaning to the indifferent universe."

In a way, it sounds a little like Christianity. "Love never fails," St. Paul says. John Paul II adds that "Hatred can only be conquered by love."[1] "Nothing is sweeter than love, nothing stronger, nothing loftier, nothing broader, nothing pleasanter, nothing fuller or better in heaven nor on earth..." Thomas à Kempis writes in *Imitation of Christ*. Woody Allen's charac-

1. https://www.vatican.va/content/john-paul-ii/en/speeches/2002/january/documents/hf_jp-ii_spe_20020110_diplomatic-corps.html

ter, Professor Louis Levy, thinks love is our shot at a meaningful life. St. Paul doesn't disagree.

But there is a big difference between the world-view Allen captures and the one put forward by the saints. The difference, in a word, is grace. You can't understand a Christian view of love without it. The story of grace and why we need it takes us back to the Garden of Eden. After God created the first humans in Genesis, he "looked at everything he had made, and found it very good." Creation had an order. Trees did what trees ought to do; bears did what they ought to do; and humans did what they ought to do. Adam's mind and heart were ordered to loving God and neighbor. When Adam and Eve committed the first sin, that order was lost. They passed the loss onto us.

Grace does two things for us. The story of the first sin points to one of them. Adam's and Eve's act of disobedience left us in state of disorder. The soul's natural powers (intellect, will, emotions) were designed to work together. Original sin made them do the opposite. The first task of grace is to restore order to the soul. It's a gift of healing that comes to us by way of the cross and gets us (mostly) back to square one.

With it comes the capacity to avoid sin, and to live in an orderly way again.

But grace also has a second job. Augustine famously said, "Our hearts are restless until they rest in you, O Lord." Happiness in the ordinary sense was not enough for him; it is not enough for us either. We have a desire for something more. Sometimes we sense it in the beauty of nature. Other times we sense it in our sorrow. It's a longing for more happiness than this life can give. God responds to this desire with an invitation to friendship. That is where the second task of grace comes in. Grace elevates us to that friendship and readies us for the supernatural. Dante provides a fitting poetic image in the Paradiso:

> Like sudden lightning scattering the spirits
> of sight so that the eye is then too weak
> to act on other things it would perceive,
> such was the living light encircling me,
> leaving me so enveloped by its veil
> of radiance that I could see no thing.
> "The Love that calms this heaven always welcomes
> into Itself with such a salutation,
> to make the candle ready for its flame."

The poet needs divine light to see divine light because his eyes are too weak on their own. The same goes for us. We require a gift of God's own life in grace to have a life with God. The light Dante receives is temporarily blinding because it is beyond what the natural eye can see. Grace is like that, too. It is beyond nature; it is supercharged. C.S. Lewis would say that it is too real. Grace makes this friendship with God possible. In the 70s and 80s Christian artists loved to depict "best bud" Jesus. The message was always more or less the same: Jesus is your Lord and Savior and he's also a good pal. He'll laugh at your jokes and buy you a beer. This kind of kitsch is mostly out of fashion now. It made for bad art and even worse theology.

One of my favorite children's books, *The Velveteen Rabbit*, helps to show what it got wrong. You may remember the story, of the loyal little stuffed bunny who remained at the side of his boy until his whiskers came off and his fur grew dull. He was destined for the fire when something magic happened: his love and loyalty made him a real bunny. The ending is a happy surprise. The point is that no one expects a stuffed bunny to become a real bunny. It takes magic or a miracle to make that happen. Friendship with God is a little like that. God is no ordinary pal. Friendship with him is an ending beyond our imagining. But it is not magic that gets us there; it is grace.

With this picture in mind, we see why the theological virtues—faith, hope, and love—have a reputation for being special. They are gifts to prepare us for this friendship. That is one reason they differ from other virtues like benevolence or chastity. Benevolence and chastity help us to be good and happy in this life. They prepare us to be good fathers and mothers, brothers and sisters, employees, citizens, and members of a community. They are measures of human goodness that apply universally. They aim at happiness in the ordinary sense. But faith, hope, and love point elsewhere. They prepare us for something beyond.

The theological virtues differ from other virtues in another way. In the last chapter I said that virtues are the result of good habits. We acquire them by repeatedly doing good actions, as we build muscles through practice. Over time they become stable dispositions in our souls. But the theological virtues are different. We cannot acquire them through our own efforts. They are pure gifts; only God can give them. Our job is to ask him to do that for us.

Like the other virtues, the theological virtues are connected to our actions. They help us to act in a way that is worthy of heaven. Just as Dante could not see the highest heaven without the gift of divine light, so we cannot act in a way deserving of heaven without the gift of the theological virtues. Aided by them, we can pursue our ultimate end, to know, love, and serve God. One of the ancient hymns of the Church puts it this way: Ubi caritas est vera, Deus ibi est. Where true charity is, God is there. When we act in faith, hope, or love a piece of heaven touches earth.

Each of the theological virtues has its own particular character. Faith comes first because hope and love logically presuppose it. It is the virtue by which we accept the truths of God's revelation. We approach scripture and church teaching with the virtue of faith. It allows us to see that God is one but three divine persons—Father, Son, and Holy Spirit—and to affirm that Jesus rose from the dead and ascended into heaven. Reason alone cannot get us there. Faith also transforms how we perceive the events of our own lives. The joy of this life looks different in the light of heavenly joy. So does suffering. C.S. Lewis offers this perspective in *The Great Divorce*: "[Mortals] say of some temporal suffering, 'No future bliss can make up for it' not knowing that Heaven, once attained, will work backwards and turn even that agony into a glory." Faith gives us this heavenly perspective while we are on earth. Through it, we might find glory in both our joy and our suffering.

Hope is our trust in God's promise of eternal life. With hope we fix our gaze on the place where our ultimate happiness lies. We cannot reach this place on our own, just as we cannot see the truth of the resurrection without faith. Hope also nurtures the assurance, given by faith, that God wants us to be in heaven with him. Like faith, hope imbues our actions with new meaning. To live in hope is to recognize that we are bound for heaven, that we are not there yet, and that we will only get there by God's grace. Hope is the virtue that allows us to fully engage with this world even as we belong to heaven. Benedict XVI says that it is hope "that gives us the courage to place ourselves on the side of good even in seemingly hopeless situations" because we put our trust not on our own goodness, but in God's.

Finally, charity is the virtue that puts God first. By charity, or love, we desire and honor God above all things and for his own sake. If faith shows us the destination, and hope gives us the confidence we can reach it, then charity is the vehicle that takes us there. Through charity we also learn how to love others as God loves them. Think of the charity of Mother Teresa, who saw the face of Christ on the poor men and women she served. In the love of God and others, we have a foretaste of the love we will experience in heaven.

These three virtues are the heart of the Christian life. Appropriately, they are also the heart of this book. Of all the virtues, they have the most profound influence over our actions. They point them toward heaven. And they bring the grace of heaven to earth. The love that might transform the world does not come from us, as Woody Allen's Professor Louis Levy would have it, but from God. It's not our task to give meaning to an indifferent universe, but to receive meaning from a God who is anything but. Only by way of God's grace can we hope to bring light to the world.

FAITH

THERE IS A POPULAR misunderstanding about the virtue of faith. It goes something like this: faith is a thing people cling to when life is too hard. It's an illusion that protects us from the truth, a kind of noble lie like the one Jack Nicholson defended in the movie *A Few Good Men*. Nicholson's character, Col. Nathan Jessup, was called to testify in a military trial about a hazing incident. "You can't handle the truth," he sneered at the young lawyer questioning him (Tom Cruise). His point was that the lawyer's faith in the Marines depended on a lie. Without the blindness of faith, he would not have been able to tolerate the harsh realities of life in the Corps.

This is how some people in our secular age think about Christian faith. Faith, they imagine, is willful blindness to the truth. St. John Paul II addressed this idea in his encyclical *Fides et Ratio*. He described faith and reason as "two wings on which the human spirit rises to the contemplation of truth." The real disagreement between skeptics and believers is not so much about faith as it is about truth. The secular view holds that truth is only what sense and reason can prove. This makes the truth pretty small.

Christianity, by contrast, holds that truth is infinite. We can't possibly expect to know it all. If we could, we would in some sense be infinite too. Much of what is true inevitably surpasses our reason. And that is where faith comes in. It is not (to use a theological phrase) an endowment of our nature, but a pure gift. It is God's way of inviting us to perceive truth beyond our ability.

Emily Dickinson said it this way:

> *Faith—is the Pierless Bridge*
> *Supporting what We see*
> *Unto the Scene that We do not—*
> *Too slender for the eye*

In Dickinson's metaphor we walk (along the bridge) rather than fly (on two wings), but like St. John Paul II, she sees faith as something that takes us to scenes we cannot see with eyes alone. Faith is not blind to the truth; it enlarges our field of vision.

Think about the special theory of relativity—the idea that mass and energy are interchangeable. I believe this is true, though I don't understand the mathematics and have no first-hand experience of their interchangeability. But Albert Einstein and other really smart people have done experiments and worked out the math. I accept the notion that $E = mc^2$ because they say so. In short, I believe something because I believe someone.

This is how it is with faith. The someone we believe is God himself, who reveals himself in scripture. St. Augustine spoke in his *Confessions* about the wisdom of the Neoplatonist philosophers. They knew, he said, that "the Word, God, was 'born not of the flesh, nor of blood ... but of God.'" But there were things their philosophizing could not disclose to them: "that 'the word was made flesh and dwelt among us,' I did not read there." The great philosophers of the ancient world perceived something of the divine, but they did not know that "God so loved the world that he gave his only Son." That truth comes only through faith in revelation.

Faith is a gift, but you still have to nourish it. Let me offer a few pieces of advice for how to do that in college. First, make a plan. If you are Catholic, go to mass on Sunday, or more often if you can. Vatican II called the eucharist the source and summit of Christian life. It was not just being poetic. Nearly every saint, from Augustine to Óscar Romero, speaks of the importance of going to mass.

Remember to pray, too, and not just when you need something. As Pope Benedict XVI wisely said, prayer keeps our friendship with God alive. If you're lucky enough to have been taught to pray by your parents, keep up the habit. If you've never prayed, college is a great opportunity to learn how. In either case, college represents a new occasion to grow in your spiritual life. From here on out, whether or not you pray is up to you. Learning to do it on your own is a big step toward fully embracing faith as an adult.

My second piece of advice is, let faith shape your work. There is an old saying, "Pray as though everything depends on God. Work as though everything depends on you." That is about right. Faith strengthens us. It helps us exceed our own expectations. It also imbues work with deeper meaning. St. Josemaría Escrivá explains why. When we put God at the center of our work, our work becomes a spiritual practice. Even when it is mundane or seemingly insignificant. In work a Christian may "find the secret, which is hidden from so many, of something great and new: Love."

On the other hand faith helps us to understand that everything does not depend on us. We owe it to God and to our fellow man to give our affairs our best effort. But in the end we hand them over to God. He does with them what he wills. Faith allows us to see that, too.

My last piece of advice is that faith is a gift to be shared. One of my favorite liturgies is the Easter Vigil. Before the congregation processes into church on Holy Saturday evening each person is handed an unlit candle. In the darkened church the flame of the Paschal candle is then used to light candles along the aisle. Each person who receives the light shares it with his neighbor, and so on until the whole church is illuminated. That is how faith works. We receive the light of Christ from others. Then we share it in our turn.

I like to remember the motto of my university, The Catholic University of America: Deus Lux Mea Est. God is my light. Many people we meet in the course of our lives will have faith. But many will not. It enlivens our own faith to share it with them.

If faith is the center of our lives, the words of poet Alexander Pope may be our own:

> Oh lead me whereso'er I go,
>
> Through this day's life or death!
> This day, be bread and peace my lot;
> All else beneath the sun,
>
> Thou know'st if best bestow'd or not,
> And let thy will be done.

HOPE

ONE OF THE LITTLE ceremonies we observe at the opening of the Olympics—along with lighting the flame and advertising the official soft drink—is releasing a flock of doves. We do this at weddings and funerals too. I remember seeing it happen in Kentucky at a Honda dealership opening. I'd love to do it at a university baccalaureate mass but it might be risky in a confined space. So what's up with the birds? Why do we feel obliged to set them free at a celebration?

As my son Michael once said, "It's symbolic, dude." This means there is some room for interpretation. So here's mine: it's about hope. This is the virtue that inspires all beginnings. We picture hope as a bird. Keats and Sandburg did; Eliot and Bronte too. My favorite is Emily Dickinson:

> *Hope is the thing with feathers*
> *That perches in the soul,*
> *And sings the tune without the words,*
> *And never stops at all,*
> *And sweetest in the gale is heard;*
> *And sore must be the storm*

That could abash the little bird
That kept so many warm.

Hope has wings because it reaches toward something beyond: in the Olympics, farther, higher, faster; at weddings, the joy of married life; at funerals, the bliss of the eternal. It seems like a simple, natural passion always turned to the On position. It's a beginning. There is no past. The future is long. There lie before us the prospects of success, fame, fortune, satisfaction; partnership, honor, election to high office, security for our loved ones.

I said that hope was a virtue. But what I have described is more like a passion. It would be odd to say that thirst was a virtue, or concupiscence. I have described how we feel—a kind of ardent longing coupled with a (qualified) expectation of fulfillment. Hope has something to do with this kind of desire, but what?

The final stanza of Dickinson's poem gives us a clue. It goes like this:

I've heard it in the chillest land,
And on the strangest sea;
Yet, never, in extremity,
It asked a crumb of me.

This is a funny twist. I've pictured hope as an impulse that "perches in the soul." But it seems to have a life of its own. And though it sings and keeps me warm, it never asks a crumb in return. This is a very different kind of bird. It's not just a wish or desire welling up from within ("I hope I get a Daisy air rifle for Christmas"; "I hope I pass the bar exam"). It is a free gift that flies in from somewhere outside.

These two aspects of hope—a desire and a gift—seem not to fit together. But I think in the end they do. Hope is one of the special virtues that comes to us by grace. Like faith and love, it is a gift. St. Thomas Aquinas says of grace that it builds on nature. Hope works in that way, too. We have a natural desire for happiness. On its own, that desire is directed toward our earthly pursuits. But transformed by grace, our desire for happiness becomes a desire for heaven.

Still, desire alone is not enough. In fact, the gift of a desire for heaven would be cruel without the assurance that we can get there. Scripture promises that desire will be fulfilled. "Let us hold fast the confession of our hope without wavering," Paul says, "for he who promised is faithful" (Hebrews 10:23). But how do we internalize that promise? How does it become a part of how we live?

Here's what I think. Hope is the virtue that connects our desire for heaven with God's promises. It links our deepest longing for happiness with God. Think of Psalm 146:

> *Happy is he ...*
> *whose hope is in the Lord his God,*
> *who made heaven and earth,*
> *the sea, and all that is in them;*
> *who keeps faith forever;*
> *who executes justice for the oppressed;*
> *who gives food to the hungry.*

Dickinson's poem is right. Hope gives the soul wings. But these are not wings to fly us in any direction we choose. They are wings that are made for heaven. Maybe that is why St. Paul uses a very different image to describe hope. He calls it the anchor of our soul. It couldn't be more unlike than the image of wings. And yet together they help bring the complexity of hope into focus. Hope is there to carry us to our final end. It gives us wings, but also keeps us from drifting. Like the other theological virtues, it tethers us to God. It is the virtue that allows us to rely on Him instead of our own power.

What does this have to do with Honda dealerships and Olympic ceremonies? Hope inspires all beginnings but it only directs us toward one end: God. The virtue of hope is not a wish for success, fame, fortune, satisfaction, partnership, honor, election to high office, even security for our loved ones. Those are fine things. But hope looks for eternal happiness.

It may sound like hope only looks to the future, but this isn't so. Think again about Emily Dickinson's bird:

> *I've heard it in the chillest land,*
> *And on the strangest sea;*
> *Yet, never, in extremity,*
> *It asked a crumb of me.*

Hope is related to charity. It never asks a crumb because it is a gift. We might infer from Dickinson's verse that we who receive it ought to have something to give. The Catechism agrees. It says that the soul transformed by hope is "preserved from selfishness and led to the happiness that flows from charity." The assurance of hope gives a foretaste of what is to come. In the words of another poet

> *This heaven has no other where than this:*
> *the mind of God, in which are kindled both*
> *the love that turns it and the force it rains.*

(Dante Paradiso, Canto XXVII)

The heaven we will experience in the hereafter is the love we have known on earth magnified. Hope connects our love now with the love we await.

CHARITY

AMERICANS ARE LONELY. We now have a Loneliness Index (developed by the health service company Cigna) to help us track just how lonely we are. A couple of years ago it reported epidemic levels. In 2020 three in five Americans (61%) said they were lonely.[2] Among workers from Generation Z (22 and under) an astounding 73% reported sometimes or always feeling alone.[3] The public opinion company YouGov added

2. Cigna surveyed 10,441 adults ages 18 and over. "Loneliness and the Workplace." Available at https://www.multivu.com/players/English/8670451-cigna-2020-loneliness-index/

3. CNBC "Loneliness is Rising and Younger Workers and Social

this sad statistic to the data pool: about one in five Millennials (23–38) say they have no friends.[4]

Things might be getting worse. Since Cigna's report the Covid-19 pandemic has exacerbated the loneliness problem. More than 93,000 Americans died from overdoses during the lockdowns, most of them opioid-related.[5] Homicides and liver disease (often related to alcohol abuse) also surged. Meanwhile the U.S. fertility rate fell to its lowest point since the 1930s. The isolation of lockdowns is only one contributing factor. But these metrics tell us something about the effects of isolation.

There are other troubling patterns linked to loneliness. Some of them are related to social media use. Facebook and Twitter were invented to make us feel more connected to one another, but they seem to be having the opposite effect.[6] Social scientists find that

Media Users Feel it Most" Available at https://www.cnbc.com/2020/01/23/loneliness-is-rising-younger-workers-and-social-media-users-feel-it-most.html

4. Psychology Today "Why Millennials are so Lonely." Available at https://www.psychologytoday.com/us/blog/compassion-matters/201909/why-millennials-are-so-lonely

5. Scientific American "Drug Overdose Deaths in 2020 Were Horrifying." Available at https://www.scientificamerican.com/article/drug-overdose-deaths-in-2020-were-horrifying/

6. NPR "Feeling Lonely? Too Much Time on Social Media May be

they have a negative impact on our well-being.[7] They also impair our ability to communicate with one another. The practice of internet trolling arose solely for the purpose of instigating conflict. It thrives on a lack of accountability. It is harder to dispense with civility face-to-face. It's also harder to lie, and trolls do plenty of that.

They are not the only ones stirring things up on the internet. Some public figures routinely exploit the volatility of social media to boost their causes. The same goes for some social movements and organizations. Even news outlets have become more inflammatory and less objective since the birth of social media.

Facebook and Instagram have a share of the responsibility for the rise in loneliness, but they are not entirely to blame. Four years before Mark Zuckerberg launched The Facebook Robert Putnam wrote a book entitled *Bowling Alone*. He observed that the thriving

Why." Available at https://www.npr.org/sections/health-shots/2017/03/06/518362255/feeling-lonely-too-much-time-on-social-media-may-be-why

7. National Library of Medicine "Association of Facebook Use with Compromised Well Being: A Longitudinal Study." Available at https://pubmed.ncbi.nlm.nih.gov/28093386/

free associations of a previous age were in rapid decline. As a result Americans were becoming increasingly lonely and disconnected. Personal interests were narrowing. Americans had begun to care more about less, and to have less in common. Groups that once brought people together, like local bridge clubs, dissolved. Solitary recreation (bowling alone) took their place. Things are worse now. Today Putnam might call his book *Gaming Alone*.

Social science sheds some light on the problem. But I think we have to look elsewhere for the solution. Genesis said that it was not good for Adam to be alone. God created Eve so that he might have a partner. From the beginning, the human race was made for love. Love of God was first; love of others came from that. God's intention for the first human family was that it be a community where love was passed from one generation to the next. Human love was meant to magnify divine love. Loneliness was not part of the plan.

But it didn't work out that way. Adam and Eve had their own ideas about what they wanted from life. Within a generation they had wrecked God's plan. They were evicted from the Garden of Paradise for violating the terms of their lease. And their oldest son Cain murdered his brother Abel. William Blake's illustration captures the way sin divides us from one another. On one side of the picture Eve weeps over the body of Abel while Adam looks on in horror and sadness. On the other side, Cain is driven away by dark clouds and a strong wind—the curse of his own jealousy. The figures of Eve, Adam, and Abel together point in one direction, Cain in the other. Blake depicts a family torn in two.

Loneliness and alienation are not sins against charity like Cain's jealousy. But like jealousy they tend to show up when charity is missing. Sometimes sin causes our alienation and loneliness, as it did for Cain. Sometimes it's the other way around. And sometimes we are alienated through no fault of our own. In all these cases what we need is the virtue of charity. It's the virtue that guides us in our common life. The Catechism says it is the source of friendship and communion. It brings us near to one another; it recalls our mutual obligations; and it reminds us that we share equally in human dignity.

So "all you need is love," as the Beatles said. It sounds easy. Why, then, is charity such a struggle?

The short answer is that it's hard. Dorothy Day spent decades working among the poor. Her charity for those she served was legendary, but not automatic. In one of her books she talks about an experience she had riding the bus in Brooklyn. All her fellow riders that day were destitute. One in particular wore a look of hopelessness. The scene brought her to tears. "I had been struck by one of those 'beams of love,'" she writes, "wounded by it in a most particular way." It was not pity that moved her. It was her own "inexcusable incapacity to love."

Day's recollection of her bus ride points to something important. Charity's demand that we love our neighbors can be uncomfortable, even unpleasant. In a world filled with sin and selfishness it's not natural. Sometimes it requires a sacrifice of personal resources. That's what almsgiving is about. Other times it requires something even more personal, like the physical sacrifice a mother makes to give life to a child. "'To love at all," C.S. Lewis said, "is to be vulnerable." Christ knew what that was like. So did Mary.

If this all sounds a little overwhelming, it should. "Charity is patient and kind, charity is not jealous or boastful; it is not arrogant or rude. Charity does not insist on its own way; it is not irritable or resentful; it does not rejoice at wrong, but rejoices in the right. Charity bears all things, believes all things, hopes all things, endures all things." This is not a virtue we can consistently practice by our own efforts. Like faith and hope, it is a gift.

First and foremost, the virtue of charity is about loving God. It grants us the privilege of his friendship. That is one reason it is the most important of the virtues. Another reason is that charity is the virtue that unites all the others. Theologians call it the form of the virtues. Without charity, St. Paul writes, we are nothing. But with charity, we experience the fullness of the Christian life.

The same grace that allows us to love God transforms how we love others. We see this in the heroism of the saints. Mother Teresa loved the poor and dying as though they were Christ himself. St. Maximilian Kolbe volunteered to take the place of a father condemned to a starvation chamber at Auschwitz. St. Thérèse found a way to love in the little challenges of her convent life. We see it in everyday holiness, too: the child who welcomes an elderly parent into his home; the parents who care for a baby with special needs; the priest who lives a humble life of service in his parish.

You'll find it in college too, if you look for it. Don't wait for it to come to you. Seek it out. Look for examples of charity in your classrooms, in your campus ministry, and among your peers. Where you find people who care about charity, you'll also find connection. You'll find God there, too.

THE CARDINAL
VIRTUES

A SERIES OF THREE PANELED frescoes decorates
the town hall of Siena, Italy (where St. Catherine lived). The panels are the work of Ambrogio Lorenzetti, painted between 1338 and 1339. Each scene
captures an aspect of good or bad government. One
panel is known as the Allegory of Good Government: a figure representing the Sienese government is
flanked on both sides by the virtues of Fortitude, Prudence, Peace, Magnanimity, Temperance, and Justice.
Wisdom hovers overhead.

Underneath the painting these words are in-
scribed:

*This holy virtue [Justice], where she rules, induces to unity
the many souls [of citizens], and they, gathered together for
such a purpose, make the Common Good [ben comune] their
Lord; and he, in order to govern his state, chooses never to*

turn his eyes from the resplendent faces of the Virtues who sit around him.

Lorenzetti makes a connection between unity and virtue in Siena. A well governed Siena is unified around the good of its citizens. Virtuous governance is the means for bringing unity about. Lose sight of the virtues, Lorenzetti warns in another fresco, and unity will be lost as well. The Effects of Bad Government on the City shows how. Nothing in the painting is as it should be. The city crumbles and a tyrant reigns. Instead of virtues, Cruelty, Deceit, Fraud, Fury, Division, War, Avarice, Pride, and Vainglory rule. The fresco itself is off-center.

The virtues that make a city good, according to Lorenzetti, are those famously set forth by Plato, St. Ambrose, St. Thomas Aquinas, and others, as the "cardinal" virtues: Fortitude, Justice, Temperance, and Prudence. Lorenzetti adds to these a couple of others (peace and magnanimity). Like the theological virtues, the cardinal virtues are meant to steer us toward happiness. But here the aim is human flourishing. The kind of happiness Lorenzetti has in mind comes from good political order. Its marks are the beauty of city architecture; the justness of city institutions; the availability of goods. Above all, its goal is thriving citizens.

The virtues of the good city, Plato observed, are also the virtues of the good soul. Lorenzetti's frescoes imply that a city which fails to cultivate the cardinal virtues will disintegrate. The same goes for the soul, according to Plato. Without virtue it lacks purpose and unity. It is pulled in different directions by its different parts. It has no order. That is why we call these the "cardinal" virtues. Cardinal means "hinge." With these virtues the moral life bends toward goodness. Without them it bends toward evil. "They make possible ease, self-mastery, and joy in leading a morally good life," the Catechism says. They also give the moral life momentum. The other virtues tend to follow when they are present. By practicing them we put our freedom in the service of goodness.

I said in the prior chapter that the theological virtues aim to keep heaven in view. The cardinal virtues do that too, but in a different way. Like the theological virtues, the cardinal virtues are given to us as a gift in baptism. Unlike the theological virtues, the cardinal virtues can also be gained through human effort. Aquinas speaks of "infused" virtues (the kind we receive in baptism) and "acquired" virtues (the kind we gain through practice). The acquired virtues are the ones Plato spoke of in *The Republic*. Their aim is human flourishing in this life. As Lorenzetti's painting suggests, they are particularly important in our life together. Political and social order depends on them. But they also allow us to thrive individually.

The infused cardinal virtues do the same, but they also prepare us for heaven. C.S. Lewis notes "We might think that the 'virtues' were necessary only for this present life—that in the other world we could stop being just because there is nothing to quarrel about[.]"[1] Heaven won't require heroic acts of justice because the order there will be perfectly just. But heaven is the kind of place where only the just will feel at home. "The point is not that God will refuse you admission to His eternal world if you have not got certain qualities," Lewis goes on to say. "[T]he point is that if people have not got at least the beginnings of those qualities inside them, then no possible external conditions could make a 'Heaven' for them[.]"[2]

---

1. C.S. Lewis, *Mere Christianity* in *The Complete C.S. Lewis Signature Classics* (New York: HarperCollins, 2002) 73.
2. *Ibid.*

Because of that, infused prudence, temperance, fortitude, and justice can look a little different than their corresponding acquired virtues. Acquired temperance aims for the mean between eating too little and eating too much. But infused temperance can also be exercised by fasting. Think of the fasts of St. Catherine of Siena or the counsel of the *Rule of St. Benedict*: "Renounce yourself in order to follow Christ (Mt 16:24; Lk 9:23); discipline your body (1 Cor 9:27); do not pamper yourself, but love fasting."[3] Fasting sounds like eating too little and missing the virtuous mean. But because it is done for love of God, fasting is temperate. Acquired fortitude aims for the mean between recklessness and cowardice. But infused fortitude can be exercised in martyrdom. Thomas More accepted death rather than endorse the illegitimate marriage of Henry VIII. Maximilian Kolbe offered to die in place of another man, a father, at Auschwitz. Neither death was reckless. Both were courageous. In each case, the martyr's deep love of God and desire for union with him widened the range of the cardinal virtues.

The most important of the cardinal virtues is prudence. "Prudence is the cause of the other virtues be-

3. Rule of St. Benedict, 4.10.

ing virtues at all," the philosopher Josef Pieper says. The virtues "achieve their 'perfection' only when they are founded upon prudence, that is to say upon the perfected ability to make right decisions." Elsewhere Pieper speaks of prudence as the virtue that connects the reality of our situation to our choices. A person is prudent when that connection is strong. When George Washington led the Continental Army across the Delaware through snow and sleet to engage the Hessian army at the Battle of Trenton, many thought him a fool. But history remembers him as courageous. That's because Washington saw what others didn't. Morale was low and the Continental Army desperately needed a victory if it was to succeed in the long term. The element of surprise was their best chance. There was risk (contrary to popular opinion, prudence is not the same as caution). But this was the path that aligned with the needs of the moment. Washington saw something that others could not. His choice was courageous because it was prudent.

Each of the remaining cardinal virtues has its own character, but all work alongside prudence. Consider courage and justice. We often think of them as the virtues of heroes. Often they are. But courage is not just about doing something brave. It's about doing something good. A show of bravery is only truly courage if it is done for a good cause. Prudence ensures that it is. "Fortitude must not trust itself," says St. Ambrose. What he means is that fortitude and prudence must always go together.

The same is true for justice. Martin Luther King, Jr. often spoke of how justice could not be at odds with the other virtues. In 1957 he wrote, "At the center of nonviolence stands the principle of love. In struggling for human dignity the oppressed people of the world must not allow themselves to become bitter or indulge in hate campaigns."[4] His point was that love and justice should never work against one another. Prudence ensures that they don't. It allows us to perceive what the good outcome is and the right way to get there.

Temperance lacks the flashiness of fortitude and justice. It is a plodding virtue, the kind you call on in little ways ten times a day. Sometimes it is boring. But without temperance it's hard to make room for the more heroic virtues. Excessive love of pleasure weighs

4. *Christian Century* 74 (6 February 1957) "Nonviolence and Racial Justice" Available here: https://kinginstitute.stanford.edu/king-papers/documents/nonviolence-and-racial-justice

us down. It makes it harder to rise to the occasion when the opportunity comes along. Like fortitude and justice, temperance works alongside prudence to decide on the appropriate means in each circumstance. Prudence looks at the facts of the situation and guides us to judge where the mean lies. Temperance helps us to choose it.

In Philippians, St. Paul exhorts us to fix our minds on what is good: "Whatever is true, whatever is honorable, whatever is just, whatever is pure, whatever is lovely, whatever is gracious, if there is any excellence, if there is anything worthy of praise, think about these things." The cardinal virtues are the means by which we live St. Paul's command. The Catechism says that living by these virtues permits us "not only to perform good acts, but to give the best of [ourselves]." At the same time, the cardinal virtues keep us on the path toward heaven. Dante pictures them as female figures who accompany an empty chariot in the Purgatorio. They keep the chariot on track from one side. On the other side are the theological virtues and the four Gospels. Together their job is to keep us near to Christ, who drives the chariot, as we navigate the challenges of this life.

PRUDENCE

THE LANDMARK CASE *Roe v. Wade* turns 50 soon. It will be a day of mourning for pro-life Americans, as it has been every year since *Roe* was decided. On the other side, pro-abortion advocates will celebrate fifty years of abortion empowering women. Evidence of the physical and psychological damage of abortion (and there's a lot of it) will be swept under the rug. Advocates won't mention that legal abortion facilitates the sex trafficking industry or the abuse of children. The loss of unborn life, male and female, won't come up either.

Pro-abortion advocates say we need to protect "freedom of choice." But they are agnostic about what we choose. We are counseled not to be judgy; not to impose our values on others. Abortion or childbirth, it's a woman's decision.

> *I do my thing and you do your thing....*
> *You are you, and I am I, and if by chance we find*
> *each other, it's beautiful.*
> *If not, it can't be helped.*

— 63 —

In this view of the world, the prudent woman knows how to get what she wants. If it's an abortion, she knows whether to take a pill, have a vacuum aspiration, D & E, induction; she knows what will be most cheap, safe, and effective. The virtue resides in the wise choice of means. The choice of ends is not the concern of the moral life. This is the first maxim of liberalism.

The plurality opinion of another landmark abortion case, *Planned Parenthood v. Casey*, distills what is behind this view of prudence: "At the heart of liberty is the right to define one's own concept of existence, of meaning, of the universe, and of the mystery of human life." Pro-life advocates often point out that such a right is abhorrent when it implies a right to snuff out the life of another. True. But there's something else rotten at the core of *Casey*'s claim. Its view of morality envisions no obligation to align our actions with what is good (which it takes to be a purely subjective matter). Instead, our task is to decide what is good for us. The prudence we seek to cultivate is purely self-serving. In fact, it looks less like prudence, and more like Nietzsche's will to power.

St. Thomas Aquinas calls this a false prudence, a

kind of "cleverness" or "cunning." We may, he says, speak of a "good robber," or even a "prudent robber, ... because he devises fitting ways of committing robbery." But true prudence "devises fitting ways of obtaining a good end." The idea is that I perceive goodness—in God, in others, and in creation—and I want to make myself more like it. Prudence serves to move me in that direction. If it moves me only toward what I want (regardless of whether it is good), it is no longer prudence. "That is prudent which is in keeping with reality," the philosopher Josef Pieper says. "Reality is my choice," Casey might reply. On that view, prudence is only the cleverness needed to make my choice a reality.

It's easy to see that false prudence of this kind is not what we ought to strive for, especially when it is used to do inherently bad things like take innocent life. But most of the moral life does not consist in resisting the inclination to do bad things. Often we are choosing between good things. The challenge for prudence is figuring out which is best under the circumstances. Here's what I mean. There was a new production of *Little Women* in the theaters a couple of years ago, with Saoirse Ronan as Jo. The novel and the film pose the question whether Jo should marry Laurie, her neighbor and good friend, or seek a career as a writer. Jo prudently recognizes that she and Laurie would not be temperamentally suited; and that her talents as a writer need a different companion to flourish.

Neither of Jo's choices was a bad thing, like killing unborn children. Both choices (marriage to a good man, a vocation as a writer) involved doing good things. In the end (spoiler alert) Jo's sister Amy marries Laurie, and we are left to think that they lived happily. But Jo's election was a real moral dilemma; it was not a matter of indifference how it came out. It's an example of the moral tension that Alasdair MacIntyre observes, "between the claims of family life and those of the arts." Aquinas says this kind of decision concerns "the good end of [one's] whole life," and making it requires the most true and perfect prudence.

Many of our prudential choices are more mundane. Exercising prudence in those cases makes it easier when the stakes are high, like Jo's. Sometimes it's easy to see what the prudent thing to do is. Driving home, you have a choice between Papa John's or Sweetgreen for dinner. Pizza for dinner is good; grilled chicken and a salad is better. Prudence perceives the good end (health) and moves you to act toward it. Seems simple enough. But more often circumstances are less straightforward. Pizza may be a better choice if that's what a host is serving; if it's free and you're on a tight budget; or if it's your birthday. In these cases, different goods are at stake (being kind to your host; saving money; celebrating). The prudent choice changes accordingly.

In real life, things are often even more complicated than this. Maybe you need extra time to study, and pizza is faster, but you're also on a diet. Or maybe you've heard that the local pizza place doesn't treat employees well and you've decided not to patronize them until they've corrected course, but it's too late to go anywhere else. Maybe you've committed to fasting but a friend surprised you with dinner. Prudence allows us to navigate this complexity, to weigh different circumstances and considerations, and to make the choice that best serves our overall good. Exercising it well requires both an understanding of the goods at stake and their importance, and a clear perspective on our circumstances.

It also supposes a degree of self-knowledge. Personal strengths and weaknesses play an important role in prudential decision-making. Sometimes we bump up against limitations and we have to grow before we can pursue certain goods. It may be well to work on the self-discipline needed to take a midnight shift at the adoration chapel, but it might not be prudent to commit to that hour every week. A six a.m. run might be a worthy aspiration for someone who dislikes morning exercise, but it might be prudent to start with a later time. Prudence also relies on the other virtues. Charting the course to a healthy dinner is the job of prudence but it also takes temperance to follow through. Prudence might tell you to look for another job but submitting your resume will still require courage.

Flannery O'Connor once commented "[T]he older I get the more respect I have for Old Prudence." I agree. All of the cardinal virtues are important for you to cultivate as a college student, but prudence is especially so. College is a time for discernment, for beginning to figure out what you ought to do with your life. It's a big choice, and one you don't want to mess up. And it will most likely be an election from among several good options. The virtue of prudence will help you. So will knowing yourself. God calls each of us

(Jo and Amy) differently. We have a moral responsibility to figure out His will, which in large part means prayerful attentiveness to God's voice. As Pope Francis recently remarked, prudence is "the virtue of the [one] who, in order to serve with wisdom, is able to … be receptive to the … Spirit." You may not always know the right path to take, but God does. Be hopeful, pray, and listen.

JUSTICE

WHEN I WAS YOUNG, the usual sequence for studying Latin, at least in the Sharon public schools, was to do Caesar in the second year, Cicero in the third, and Virgil in the fourth. It is surprising how fast these guys have dropped from view—as fast as Latin itself has disappeared from the curriculum. A hundred years ago Cicero, in particular, was the epitome of high rhetorical style—the long flowery sentences with the verb at the end. It's a good thing we don't do this anymore. I don't like it any better than I do Victorian furniture or Romantic music.

But Cicero's essays and letters were not, as I recall, as ornate and flowery as his orations. One of them in particular, *De Officiis* (On Duties), takes the form of a letter written by Cicero to his son Marcus, then a young man of 21 and studying philosophy at the Peripatetic School in Athens. Marcus spent more time partying than studying, a lifestyle his father abetted by giving him too large an allowance. Perhaps the letter is an effort to atone for this mistake. Or it may be a reflection on the circumstances of Cicero's own life. You may recall that Cicero opposed Caesar's decision to abolish the Senate and make himself emperor. For this he was exiled. When Caesar was murdered in 44 B.C. Cicero again chose the wrong side. He opposed Antony and was killed for it. The essay On Duties comes from this period, when Cicero was banned from public life and sought the consolation of philosophy.

Book I is a discussion of the Stoics' four cardinal virtues—prudence, justice, fortitude, and temperance. And the line I want to call to your attention appears in the treatment of justice: *Non nobis solum nati sumus* ("We are not born for ourselves alone"). This is a more generous statement than the modern liberal conception ("Equal treatment for all"), for two reasons. One is that it views justice not as a debtor-creditor relationship (I owe you equal treatment), but as a virtue

(I should help you because that is a good way for me to behave). The other is its teleological flavor: being born is not something that just happens; we are born for a purpose.

It might not be immediately apparent, but there is actually a straight line that connects Cicero to us today. His emphasis on the hand of God and the virtue of justice appealed to Christian writers both early and late. St. Ambrose wrote his own *De Officiis* around 386. Renaissance humanists were fond of quoting his *Non nobis solum nati sumus.* And the most lasting adherents to the humanistic tradition of education—the Jesuits—opened their first school in Messina, Italy in 1548 with an emphasis on the same theme. I do not doubt that Cicero was taught at Messina. And from then down to the present the Jesuit motto in education has been "to form men and women for others"—we are not born for ourselves alone. Here is how Pedro Arrupe, the Superior General of the Jesuit Order, put it in 1973:

Today our prime educational objective must be to form men and women for others; men and women who will live not for themselves but for God ... ; men and women who cannot even conceive of love of God which does not include love for the least of their neighbors; men and women completely convinced that the love of God which does not issue in justice for men and women is a farce.

We should be ready to put those words into action—love God, love the least of your neighbors, do justice. These are the most important things. Not that I condemn worldly success, which can be a worthy crown of our efforts. But it must not be a target. Money, honor, office, power—anyone will go off the rails if he wants these things for their own sakes. They may come your way, and it's fine if they do. But they will not make you a better or happier person, and they will not save your soul. Love God, love the least of your neighbors, do justice.

Fans of Cicero will recall that he has a bit part in Shakespeare's *Julius Caesar*. In Act I Mark Antony offers Caesar the crown three times, and Caesar refuses—each time more reluctantly than the last. Casca is recounting these events to Cassius (I picture Edmond O'Brien and John Gielgud in that old Joseph Mankiewicz movie), and their exchange goes like this:

Cassius: Did Cicero say any thing?

Casca: Ay, he spoke Greek.

Cassius: To what effect?

Casca: Nay, an I tell you that, I'll ne'er look you i' the face
again: but those that understood him smiled at one an-
other and shook their heads; but for mine own part, it
was Greek to me.

English departments have spilled a lot of ink speculating what Cicero might have said. But I'll tell you what he said. Caesar really wanted the gold crown. And Cicero believed that would be the worst thing—for himself, for the Senate, for Rome, and for Caesar. Caesar was killed the year Cicero wrote *De Officiis*. I don't speak Greek, but I'll translate it for you. He said, "We are not born for ourselves alone. We should be men and women for others."

COURAGE

FORTITUDE, or as we now say, courage, is the kind of virtue that makes you think big. It brings to mind leaders and heroes: George Washington, Joan of Arc, Martin Luther King, Jr., Winston Churchill. These are all luminaries from whom we have a lot to learn. But here I want to reflect on two stories about my mom.

My father died of a heart attack at one o'clock in the morning, in bed with my mother, soon after their 50th wedding anniversary. We seven surviving children were grown and living around the world. At 6:30 the next morning Mom called and said, "Dear, your father died last night." Just like that. We all flew home and found ... Mother in charge. We ate dinner, sat in the living room and laughed; Mother led us in the rosary. Then she said, "John, get me a scotch. I can't understand why I feel so tired."

When she was about 80 we decided that Mom needed to move in with one of us. We all volunteered, but by common consent Annette got the honors. It meant moving to Denver, far from our home in Pennsylvania. Mother's favorite place in the world was a little cottage there, where her children grew up and where she continued to live every summer. My brother Denis told me about taking Mom up to the lake for the last time one autumn day. She poked around her old flower beds, took a last look off the dock, then squared her shoulders and got in the car.

So, what's my point? Courage is not just for epic

adventures, for generals, saints, and heroes. Everyone needs courage to live well. And not just in life's big moments. We need courage in small and ordinary ones too.

Mom didn't start being courageous the day my dad died, or the day she moved away from our family home forever. She practiced courage by getting out of bed each morning to build a home and to raise us well. She learned fortitude in the ordinary challenges. When the time came to show us how to be courageous in hard moments, it came naturally.

How does one be courageous? Start small. Have the courage to get out of bed and pray before work, even if people think that's weird. Go against the culture when it's wrong about dating and sex and love. Don't lose your dedication to the poor even if your coworkers don't get it. Talk about God—it will take guts but you'll be surprised at how many people want to hear what you have to say. Treat people as Christ would.

The small moments will ready you for bigger challenges—the kind that define your character. Each of us has a different path. What courage looks like differs accordingly. In politics and public service, for instance, the line between self-interest and duty is often blurred. Campaign advisors often say the first job of a politician is to get reelected. Doing the right thing might hurt your chances of that. If all you care about is serving another term it won't matter. But if you care about doing what is right, political success will be secondary. It takes courage to order your priorities in that way.

Things work a little differently in business. There's an old Christmas movie called *It's a Wonderful Life*. If you haven't seen it, you should. It still makes the lists of the greatest movies of all time. It says something important about the kind of courage you need in business. The story is about George Bailey who gives up the opportunity to travel the world in order to run his father's lending business. The life he chooses has fewer adventures than the one he'd hoped for. But in its own way it requires greater courage:

Just remember this, Mr. Potter, that this rabble you're talking about … they do most of the working and paying and living and dying in this community. Well, is it too much to have them work and pay and live and die in a couple of decent rooms and a bath? Anyway, my father didn't think so. People were human beings to him. But to you, a warped, frustrated old man, they're cattle.

In business, the battles fought by courage are often on behalf of human dignity. George Bailey's virtue is that he remembers that a business is meant to serve. Making money is important but not if it comes by way of hurting others. Paying employees a living wage, competing honestly to win a contract, or engineering to avoid health risks all impose costs. Opting to dignify workers and compete honestly may diminish profits and upset shareholders. It may cost you a bonus or even a job. It might be easy to give yourself an out and say "well, that's business," but it wouldn't be courageous.

In the early days of the Covid-19 pandemic the medical professions showed us another kind of courage. Doctors and nurses took risks to care for patients sick with an unknown disease. They donned heavy Personal Protective Equipment for long shifts and faced the uncertainty of whether it would be enough to prevent exposure. It was a moment that called for some heroism, and they deserved the national recognition they received. Sometimes courage in medicine is like that.

But there's a different kind of courage in the medical profession that gets less attention. It is the kind of courage it takes to deliver devastating news to a family, to face another patient after one has just been lost, or to finish out a draining shift. More than any other profession, the work of doctors and nurses touches on life and death. Medical professionals are with us in life's most vulnerable moments: when we are newly born; when we are sick; when we are injured; or when we are dying. They are witnesses to our joy and relief; more often, though, they are witnesses to our worst pain and suffering. More than anyone else, they are tasked with respecting the dignity of all stages of life. It takes courage to face all that, day in and day out.

It is fitting that most students read Socrates's *Apology* in the first or second year of college. It teaches an important lesson about the relationship between courage and truth. From that text they learn that Socrates has landed in prison for teaching an unpopular truth. Later he would be put to death for it. Without Socrates's courage, however, there would have been no Plato (he was Socrates's student). There may have been no Thomas Aquinas. At very least, his theology would have looked different.

When we think about courage in academia or in the sciences, we should keep Socrates in mind. We are lucky that today the consequences for holding fast to an unpopular truth are less dramatic. But speaking the truth still requires courage. This is especially the case for people of faith. There is no field where God is more absent than the sciences, where religious belief is often caricatured or dismissed as irrational. Believers might risk their professional reputation by living their faith. Going against this tide requires the kind of courage and intellectual integrity Socrates had.

Something similar is true in other academic settings. Colleges and universities are plagued by cynicism, suspicion, and skepticism. They favor tearing ideas down over understanding them. Some people like to claim that deconstructing is courageous. I think that's taking the easy way out. Deconstructing an idea isn't hard. It is defending one that requires real skill, and real courage. And that's my point: truth requires courage. Faith requires even more. But it is worth it. Speaking the truth in courage gives others the strength to do the same. And it has an impact on the young minds who are listening.

Finally, courage is as necessary outside of the office as in it, maybe even more. More than ever, one's personal vocation, whatever it is, requires courage. At one time the choice to become a priest or to take religious vows earned you respect and deference. Today that is no guarantee. Dedicating your life to service and embracing all the sacrifices that go with it require courage, especially at a time when commitment isn't highly regarded.

Something similar is true for those contemplating a family. We live in a culture that sees marriage as temporary and children as accessories. Going against that trend and making a commitment for life takes nerve. Once you are a parent, you have to teach courage as well as practice it. We learned about courage every day we spent with Mother. She showed us what courageous faith is, how to be a courageous parent, and how to grow old with courage. It's one of the greatest gifts she gave us. Start preparing to give that gift now. Live courageously. You won't regret it.

TEMPERANCE

AMONG THE FOUR cardinal virtues, I would venture to say, temperance is the hardest to get excited about. The other three—courage (fortitude), good judgment (prudence), and justice—are the qualities of heroes. Courage belongs to Achilles and Henry V. Prudence is the virtue of great leaders like Abraham Lincoln. Justice belongs to those like Martin Luther King who fight heroically for what is fair.

Temperance is a little less edgy. It is the virtue of a person who goes to bed on time, eats well portioned meals, and consumes alcohol in moderation. It is the virtue of the person who leaves the party at a reasonable hour, and who never gets his money's worth at the all-you-can-eat buffet. It is sought by the monk who follows in the footsteps of St. Benedict. He wrote that "moderation [should be] observed in all things." Fulton Sheen tells us temperance is the virtue we need "because our needs are limited, but our wants are unlimited."

So temperance is kind of boring. It doesn't inspire epic poems or Arthurian tales. But if you practice it, it will change your life for the better. Here's why.

First, like all the virtues it is related to happiness. This might surprise you. Temperance isn't a virtue we tend to get excited about. In fact, it has a reputation for being a killjoy. It's the inner voice that tells you not to have another piece of cake or to get to bed early. It was the rallying cry of the Prohibitionists. "The lips that touch liquor shall never touch mine," declared one Prohibitionist song. It's hard to see the fun in any of that.

Part of the difficulty is the connection between temperance and restraint. Raphael's elegant depiction of temperance in *The Cardinal and Theological Virtues* sits in the Apostolic Palace in Rome. Temperance stretches her hand out offering a bridle of restraint to all who wish to be virtuous. It's probably not a favorite image for the thousands of tourists and pilgrims heading out for gelato and wine. Raphael's depiction of temperance is on the mark. Temperance is meant to stop us from going too far. It entails a degree of restraint. But restraint and temperance are not the same. In fact, restraint isn't even what is most important. Enjoyment is.

Let me explain what I mean. We are supposed to take pleasure in good things. That is God's wish for us. What a bleak world it would be if we couldn't enjoy a well-cooked steak, a sonorous poem, or good whiskey. The trouble is that these pleasures can also be powerful. They can take up too much space in our lives. They can even control us. Temperance is the virtue that helps us to deal with that. The temperate person enjoys a steak on the right occasion but resists the urge to have it every night. He takes pleasure in a glass of whiskey without finishing the bottle. Through restraint he learns enjoyment.

Second, temperance is related to success. If you review a list of vices rather than virtues, you will find that most of them are about wanting too much stuff. The same goes for the seven deadly sins. I'd say five are failures to exercise temperance: covetousness, lust, gluttony, envy, sloth. One way of looking at the ill effects of these vices and sins is that they slow you down. Have you ever tried to work, or go for a run, or do anything (other than watch football) after Thanksgiving dinner? There's a reason we feast like that only once or twice a year. If we did it every day, nothing would ever get done. Many things we do to excess work in a similar way. Excessive drinking and partying leave us sluggish the next day. Watching just one more episode of your favorite show wastes an afternoon (there's a reason we call it "bingeing"). It's similar with gaming. Even excessive exercise can be damaging to health and a distraction from other priorities. When we allow one or more of these pleasures to become too powerful, it occludes other goods in our lives. This is especially true of goods that require discipline and restraint, and those are the goods often connected to success.

Third (and this is connected to the last two), temperance is important for building strong relationships. Marriage, friendships, parenthood, relations in the workplace—all come with responsibilities. The health of the relationship depends on you doing your part. Behavior that is excessive—drinking, eating, spending too much—undermines your ability to act responsibly. Relationships suffer as a result. Sebastian Flyte is a character from Evelyn Waugh's *Brideshead Revisited* who illustrates the point. Sebastian's love of fine food and alcohol is charming in his youth. But as he ages, these loves enslave him. His decline from a vibrant college student to a dying alcoholic in early middle age is a tragedy. Worse still is the decline of his relationships with friends and family. Some friends remain true to him but only from a distance. Sebastian's family loves him but he prefers isolation to their moralizing. Waugh finds hope for Sebastian—grace abounds even in the darkest places—but Sebastian's tragic end reveals the high cost of intemperance for relationships.

It's not only interpersonal relationships that are hurt by an excessive love of pleasure. Intemperance can also derail our relationship with God. I said a minute ago that it is good to enjoy the pleasures of creation. God made us with that in mind. But pleasures can easily become idols. They can make it difficult to find space for God. John of the Cross instructs that

> *To come to enjoy what you have not*
> *You must go by a way in which you enjoy not.*

Setting other pleasures at the margins helps us to pursue the pleasure we ought to seek most: closeness to God. That's why the mystics and monks often avoid pleasure (temporarily, at least). Temperance keeps that goal in sight and our love of pleasure in check. Pleasure can interfere with spiritual growth in other ways, too. God is like an artist, C.S. Lewis says. "The blows of his chisel, which hurt us so much, are what make us perfect." Suffering is not good in itself; we needn't seek it out. But when it finds us, it often leads to spiritual growth. Pleasure can be where we turn for comfort. It's understandable—no one likes to hurt. Temperance helps us to resist that dependence, and to rely on God instead.

None of this means life is no fun for a temperate person. Part of mastering temperance is learning when it's appropriate to indulge and when it's better to abstain. Having an extra beer on Christmas is a good idea. Drinking at a work lunch may cost you your job. The key to temperance is learning to direct your desires toward your overall goal. As Fulton Sheen says, "happiness comes from self-possession through temperance, not from self-expression through license."

THE LITTLE
VIRTUES

I F YOU VISIT THE VATICAN LIBRARY, you'll pass
through Sistine Hall (not to be confused with the
chapel of the same name). Painted by Cesare Nebbia
and Giocanni Guerra and the painters of their work-
shop in the sixteenth century, it is especially known
for its ornate ceiling. One critic refers to it as the vault
of heaven. Along one wall are frescoes of various li-
braries famous throughout history. Another wall depicts the ecumenical councils. The pillars feature
theologians, scholars, and biblical figures. The saints
appear in ornamented crosses. Rings of angels come
bearing the great texts of the ancient world. The great
monuments of Rome connect heaven to earth.

Historically Sistine Hall served as a reading room
for the library. But Nebbia and Guerra's elaborate frescoes might seem a little ill suited to that purpose. It is
hard to avoid getting caught up in their lavish scenes.

Like the ornate Baroque churches of Rome, Sistine Hall has a very Catholic feel. For Catholics, it is not the devil but God who is in the details. Our art is ornate because creation is like that, and every aspect of it reflects the glory of God. "[T]he entire universe, with all its parts, is ordained towards God as its end, inasmuch as it imitates, as it were, and shows forth the Divine goodness, to the glory of God," Aquinas says. All of creation is a rich tapestry. Each perfection of the universe reveals God's goodness in a unique way.

Something similar is true of the moral life. The theological and cardinal virtues are its centerpiece. As Dante's image of the chariot shows, together they make us followers of Christ and steer us in the direction of heaven. But other virtues work alongside these seven. They are more ordinary and humble. St. Francis de Sales calls them "little virtues" in his *Introduction to the Devout Life*. Most of us do not have regular occasion to exercise the flashier virtues like strength, magnanimity, or magnificence, he notes, but the subtler ones like gentleness, modesty, and humility are "graces which ought to color everything we do." Moreover, the saint advises, "it is well to have a good and ready stock in hand of those general virtues of which we stand in so perpetual a need."

The littleness of these virtues does not make them unimportant. St Thérèse has the smallness of her own soul in mind when she writes, "I understood how all the flowers He has created are beautiful, how the splendor of the rose and the whiteness of the lily do not take away the perfume of the little violet or the delightful simplicity of the daisy." The same is true of the littleness of these virtues. Their smallness does not make them less important or beautiful. Each reflects God's goodness in its own way.

For St. Thérèse, humility was paramount. Others highlight the importance of different little virtues. Aristotle included wittiness and liberality in his enumeration of the virtues; Ben Franklin, cleanliness and tranquility. Hildegard of Bingen exalted victory and discretion in her *Ordo Virtutem*. Constancy is a top priority in Jane Austen's moral universe. Different walks of life may account for this variation. Aristotle's liberality (along with magnanimity and magnificence, which he also lists) has an aristocratic feel. Franklin's cleanliness feels democratic by comparison. Discretion must have been important for keeping healthy relationships between the religious sisters in Hildegard's convent. Constancy anchored Jane Austen's heroines through the vicissitudes of courtship at a time when women were beginning to have more say over whom they married and why.

The chapters that follow group these virtues under the headings of Youth, Middle Age, and Old Age. This division is not de Sales's, but it does comport with an idea he articulates about the virtues as fitted to one's vocation or situation in life. "Every calling stands in special need of some special virtue," he writes.

[T]hose required of a prelate, a prince, or a soldier, are quite different; so are those beseeming a wife or a widow, and although all should possess every virtue, yet all are not called upon to exercise them equally, but each should cultivate chiefly those which are important to the manner of life to which he is called.

No virtue ill suits any of us. The point, rather, is that some seem to be more relevant or more in need of work at one time or another of our lives. Younger people do well to focus on studiousness, for example, while older people are often in a better position to exercise generosity and mercy. These are generalities. Even so, there is some truth to them.

The virtues included in this section are also connected to the life of the university student. Some, like studiousness, honesty, industriousness, truthfulness, and docility, facilitate classroom learning. They help students get the most out of their study. Others, like silence and constancy, are foundational for the spiritual life. Patience, generosity, and hospitality are virtues we tend to focus on in middle age, but they also help students to cultivate productive relationships with their peers. Humility, meekness, modesty, and gentleness are the virtues that allow for healthy disagreement in and out of the classroom. They allow differences of opinion to facilitate growth, rather than division. Mercy, magnanimity, and benignity may be more characteristic of old age, but they are also important to young friendships. Repentance is too, above all in a student's friendship with God. Wisdom and joy are important to all ages of life.

These little virtues may not be quite as important

as charity and courage. But they strengthen and support the cardinal and theological virtues. They bring goodness into small, everyday things. Like the subtle details of Sistine Hall, they enrich life's overall beauty. Each of them has a role to play in supporting the bigger pieces of the moral life. But each also has its own beauty and perfection.

YOUTH

IT IS SAID that youth is wasted on the young. I don't think that's quite right. Here's something closer to the truth: youth is appreciated most by those who are no longer young. When you hit middle age, you have learned to slow down and appreciate moments as they come. But the young are always looking forward to what is coming next. Langston Hughes put it this way in his poem *Youth*:

> *We have to-morrow*
> *Bright before us*
> *Like a flame*
> *Yesterday, a night-gone thing*
> *A sun-down name*
>
> *And dawn to-day*
> *Broad arch above the road we came,*
> *We march.*

The tendency to look forward can lessen your appreciation of youth when you're in it. But, as Hughes suggests, it is also what is beautiful about youth. Tomorrow is always "bright before us." There is a promise of something better on the horizon. For Hughes that kind of optimism builds resilience. That is why it is the young who march forward with each dawn.

John Paul II saw something similar in youth. He connected it to a desire for truth. He wrote, "Man asks himself [existential] questions throughout his life. But in the time of youth they are particularly urgent, indeed insistent." Young people are hungry for meaning and purpose. They are willing to work hard to find it. That's one reason you'll find so many young people on college campuses looking to "give back."

Plato reminds us in the *Republic* that youth has its weaknesses too. The young have not accumulated the experience necessary to see the big picture. Often, they are just beginning to assess what is important in life. They are still learning to judge prudently and to value the truth. That optimism is often a good thing. But it can easily translate to overconfidence.

Later in life, many of us cringe at a few of the opinions we held as sophomores. Passion without judgment is easily misguided, and passions can be stubborn. The poet Christina Rosetti writes that "years must pass before a hope of youth/Is resigned utterly." Enthusiasm is not a good substitute for wisdom.

But I think John Paul II is closer to the truth. Young people have an eagerness to do something good with their lives, and a willingness to dedicate themselves to it. Their passion needs guidance; but if they have it, they offer something irreplaceable. They have energy and drive unique to their state in life. They have not yet fallen prey to cynicism and despair. They value authenticity. They seek out "those who radiate life," Pope Francis says. They are searching for something real. They don't fatigue easily.

The following chapters examine the virtues that young people, even more than their elders, need to cultivate: docility, humility, honesty, industriousness, studiousness, modesty, and silence. At this stage of life we devote a lot of our time to learning. This requires an open mind. It also demands industry and a dedication to study. Above all, it requires knowing that you have a lot of growing to do. The properly receptive attitude is characterized by humility, modesty, and the silence to hear what others have to say.

HUMILITY

I WANT TO COMMEND a condign virtue for over-achievers: humility. This virtue is often misunderstood, so there is value in taking some time to reflect on it.

First: don't confuse humility with self-deprecation. It's no virtue to deny that you have talent, or pretend your gifts do not matter. God's own mother said about herself "all generations shall call me blessed." Remember, though, what she said before: "My soul proclaims the greatness of the Lord." Mary was not boasting about her accomplishments, but about what God had done through her.

Remember also Jesus's parable of the talents. It's about the guy who went on a trip and entrusted his property to his servants. He gave five talents to one, who invested them and made five more. He gave two to another, and he also doubled down. But the servant who got one buried it in the ground and got busted on the master's return. The point is that God made your talents. He doesn't expect you to deny they exist or hide them from the world. On the contrary: He expects you to use them in his service. Ad majorem

Dei gloriam, the Jesuits say. All we do, whether great or small, is for the glory of God. The "Little Way" of St. Thérèse was humble. So were the great deeds of Joan of Arc.

Second: showing humility in the presence of others means valuing their gifts and talents—even when you think they're not so great. "We must not esteem by pretending to esteem," Augustine says, "but we should in truth think it possible for another person to have something that is hidden to us and whereby he is better than we are ...." In other words, you might not see that someone else's gifts are as good as your own, but the problem might be with your vision. Only God has perfect vision. Only he knows the whole story.

There is another gospel story that illustrates this point perfectly—the one about the poor widow who brings two coins to donate to the temple treasury (like the guy next to you at mass who empties the change from his pockets at the collection). Compared with the wealthy donors who contribute large sums, her gift seems small. But Jesus says "this poor widow put in more than all the other contributors to the treasury. For they have all contributed from their surplus wealth, but she, from her poverty, has contributed all she had, her whole livelihood." We don't know what God has granted. We don't have the wisdom to read hearts, or see God's purposes. We should learn to appreciate everyone's contribution and let God sort out the rest.

Third: humility defines your relationship with God. Aquinas says that true humility is acting in accordance with the knowledge that we are creatures and God is the Creator. Pride is its opposite. Pride, C. S. Lewis says, is a spiritual cancer. Lucifer got where he is by being proud. So humility has to be at the center of our relationship with God. But again, humility before God, like humility with others, is not about believing we are all bad. On the contrary, it is about believing we are good; but good because God made us so. Emily Dickinson captures it best in her poem *Love's Humility*:

> My worthiness is all my doubt,
>   His merit all my fear,
> Contrasting which, my qualities
>   Do lowlier appear;

Lest I should insufficient prove
    For his beloved need,
The chiefest apprehension
    Within my loving creed.

So I, the undivine abode
    Of his elect content,
Conform my soul as 't were a church
    Unto her sacrament.

True humility leads us to seek out God's help. It allows us to believe that we will find it in the simplicity of the Eucharist and confession. But humility also assures us that the sacraments will heal us, and that with God's help we can do great things. That is its paradox. We are not divine, but God has chosen to make his home with us. The best we can do is to remember that, and be grateful for it.

HONESTY

AS A LAWYER, I have come to know that two things make the difference between good and bad lawyers. One is hard work, and the other is honesty. St. Ives is the patron saint of lawyers. He died on May 19, 1303 in

Brittany. Butler's *Lives of the Saints* records about him the first lawyers' joke, and it goes like this:

> *Sanctus Ivo erat Brito*
> *Advocatus et non latro*
> *Res miranda populo.*

There is a reason why people make jokes about lawyers' honesty, and it is not that we are less honest than the average guy. Quite the contrary. The point of the jokes is that people hire lawyers on account of their honesty, and a breach of that trust is the worst disservice one can do to one's client. The dishonest lawyer is like Motel in *Fiddler on the Roof*—the tailor who can't see. Or like Dr. Kevorkian—the physician who extinguishes life. It's not true that tailors are more myopic than the rest of us; nor that doctors care less about life. Motel and Kevorkian stand out because they lack the qualities we engage them for. So too with a dishonest lawyer: the thing that people marvel at (*res miranda populo*) is that she could miss the very point of her calling.

And honesty is the point. This is one of those forests so big that we can overlook it in our focus on the trees of lawyering. Trials search for truth—Did

D kill V? Did M conspire in restraint of trade? Deals are promises—I will do this for you if you do that for me. Prospectuses are representations—Company C shipped a thousand containers last year. Trusts are aptly named. In each of these activities the lawyer speaks and writes for her client. Her business is all words. Lawyers are good at that. We're not always smarter than our clients. But what we have to offer them is this: we know what the rules are—about taxes, the environment, payment systems, stock fraud—and we know how to steer people through them, in their filings, oaths, promises, representations, trusts. All words. Our job is to speak them truly to and for our clients.

Don't make the mistake of thinking that it's just lawyers for big companies who are tempted to shade the truth. Extremism in defense of any cause can be a vice. We all condemn tax fraud. But it's also wrong to lie in order to save wetlands or spotted owls, or to stave off deportation. Indeed I think the temptation is greater when the justice of our cause lets us make peace with our consciences for ignoring little things—a misleading word here, an omission there, a failure to correct. "Why should I be punctilious," we tell ourselves, "when my zealous honesty just improves the odds that the spider will once again triumph over Miss Muffet?" This is the lamentable pride of the righteous—the belief that we are excused from the ordinary rules when our cause is just.

My mother always told me that honesty is the best policy. That's not exactly right. It's often good policy to tell the truth. A lawyer, or any professional, for that matter, with a reputation for honesty is one whom others will believe when the chips are down. A client who keeps his word is a good business partner. But the reality is sometimes it doesn't pay. We should recognize that and be honest even then. Especially then.

DOCILITY

IT IS IMPORTANT to evaluate the arguments of others, and our own, with a critical eye. Long before Paul Ricoeur coined the term "hermeneutics of suspicion" to describe the spirit of Freud and Nietzsche, St. Augustine observed that "[a]ll sin is a lie." Augustine knew that our tendency to elevate ourselves above God distorts our perception of reality.

Critical thinking helps us evaluate the wisdom of

the world. But it can discard truth along with false-hood. It's fashionable today to deconstruct all ideas as the products of prejudice—Marxist or capitalist, conservative or liberal. We think it sophisticated to examine a thinker's ulterior motives. The will to truth, Nietzsche says, is really just the will to power. But the danger of maintaining a critical distance from all ideas is that it doesn't allow us to get close to the truth.

Just as important as critical thinking in the life of the mind is the old-fashioned virtue of docility. Docility comes from the Latin word *docere*, to teach. Literally, it means to be teachable. It's the habit of being open to learning from others.

Aristotle, and St. Thomas, rightly observed that docility is a practical necessity. We can't be experts in all things, so when it comes to making decisions we have to trust the wisdom of others. When we are sick we trust doctors to diagnose our ailments. When we are lost, we ask locals for directions. When you file your taxes for the first time, you need the advice of a parent; when you get older you need a CPA.

Aristotle thought it was particularly important to listen to the wisdom of the old. When we choose a course of action we need to know the facts of the matter and the goal we should have in mind. We learn these things from experience, not textbooks. "Therefore," the Philosopher says in the *Ethics*, "we ought to attend to the ... sayings and opinions of experienced and older people[;] because experience has given them an eye to see aright."

We become wiser by learning from those with more experience. That is as true of the dead as of the living. G.K. Chesterton once said that "[t]radition means giving votes to the most obscure of all classes, our ancestors. It is the democracy of the dead." If we are wise ourselves, we know that we have much to learn from those who have gone before us. Docility opens us to receiving that wisdom. It quiets the pride that might otherwise lead us to think we are superior. It allows us to approach the words of Homer and St. Augustine with humility.

Chesterton also said, "Democracy tells us not to neglect a good man's opinion, even if he is our groom; tradition asks us not to neglect a good man's opinion, even if he is our father." In a culture as technologically advanced as ours, it's easy to fall into the trap of believing that we are smarter than everyone else. Progress does not make us wiser or more just. Often it does the opposite. Docility helps us to remember that the most important lessons have been learned and re-learned throughout history. We would do well to listen to them.

That is not to say that docility requires blind obedience. The child who believes his mother when she says the stove is hot is not a dupe. His experience has taught him that his mother loves him and her word can be trusted. We call the University our "alma mater" (our nourishing mother) because we trust that our professors are feeding us the truth. We call the Church our Mother for similar reasons. We put our trust in her because we find truth in the words of Christ. That trust is vindicated when our experience of the world aligns with what we have been taught.

And maybe that's the most important point about docility. We all have a lot to learn. Don't be such a skeptic that you set to one side the accumulated wisdom of the world. Just be careful in choosing your teachers.

SILENCE

SILENCE IS a sort of temperance, the cardinal virtue that moderates the appetites. This might seem a little odd at first. I wouldn't have thought that we have an appetite for talking, as we do for drink (think of the Women's Christian Temperance Union), and food (think of Overeaters Anonymous), and sex. Silence is the ability to bite your tongue, but where's the compulsion there?

Where indeed. Today we lack the ability to hold back our thumbs. Facebook and Twitter, email and Instagram, TikTok and WhatsApp are an obsession, particularly among the young. One recent survey reported that 73% of its respondents admit to using their phones even while in the bathroom.[1] Much of that activity is dedicated to social media. If you doubt that it's an appetite, think about how it can compete with activities in the traditional lineup. People cook meals not to eat them or feed their families, but to photograph them for sharing on social media.

---

1. https://www.prnewswire.com/news-releases/93-of-young-people-admit-to-using-their-phones-on-the-toilet-according-to-new-survey-301302005.html

Benjamin Franklin ranked silence second on the list of thirteen virtues he thought essential to live a good life. "Speak not but what may benefit others or yourself; Avoid trifling Conversation," he advised. Today he might say, "Tweet not but what may benefit others."

Practicing silence doesn't mean never to speak. In the counterculture of the 1960s, the "sound of silence" was a bad thing. It meant turning a deaf ear to injustice or suffering. "Silence like a cancer grows," Paul Simon writes in *The Sound of Silence*. The kind of silence he's talking about has more in common with the noise of social media than the silence of St. Benedict. Turning a deaf ear to injustice or suffering often results from being distracted. St. Benedict's silence makes space for the truth to be heard and for injustice to be recognized.

That's why St. Francis de Sales wisely suggests that silence isn't about limiting the quantity of your words, but making sure that what you say is useful.

The silence, so much commended by wise men of old, does not refer so much to a literal use of few words, as to not using many useless words. On this score, we must look less to the quantity than the quality, and, as it seems to me, our aim should be to avoid both extremes.

That's a good rule to govern our social behavior. We will profit one another more if we speak less often and more thoughtfully. But it's not the only point in controlling our compulsion to tweet. St. Benedict knew something about this. He wrote the book on being quiet, and for him silence was not just about good social relations and effective communication.

Silence, Benedict maintained, is the prerequisite for true self-knowledge, the doorway to our encounter with God. He held it in such high esteem that he advised that even when you have something good to say, you should err on the side of not saying it. This is foreign to modern ears. Fr. Patrick Barry, in his book on Benedict's Rule, makes this observation about why silence is so important, not just for monks, but for the rest of us:

Mankind in the twentieth century set out to fathom everything, understand everything, control everything in the world including the human race and its destiny. This has led to achievements that in some respects have been and continue to be amazing and beneficial. Yet at the height of these achievements, men and women are haunted by ignorance of self: 'Who am I? What is my life for?' Monastic life is different. It does not have all the answers, but it has preserved one invaluable piece of wisdom about the way to find answers. To know oneself one must withdraw, at least for a time, from the incessant din of life.

He continues:

There is a special reason for silence in a monastery. It is a reason that has its meaning for laity also. It is the very condition for truly seeking God.... It is [in] Christ's silent confrontation with each of us that we become truly ourselves and suddenly discover in him who we really are.

It is good that our lives are filled with activity. But we must make sure to leave some room in our schedules for silence, for reflection, and for God.

MODESTY

WE USE THE WORD "modesty" to describe a lot of different things—dress, comportment, thought. And whatever we mean by it, it's usually not something good. We encourage our friends not to be so modest.

(We wouldn't say that about courage or justice.) At best, modesty seems boring. Aquinas says it's the virtue that moderates "lesser" and "ordinary" matters. At worst, modesty seems an excuse for failure. Nietzsche calls it a negative consequence of "slave morality," which casts down the mighty and lifts up the lowly.

Perhaps it's fitting that modesty so demurely hides its greatness.

Consider Fanny Price. The modest protagonist of *Mansfield Park* may be the least likeable of Jane Austen's heroines. She's not witty like Elizabeth Bennet, or charming like Emma Woodhouse. Fanny won't take part in a play her cousins put on, because it puts the characters in compromising situations "unfit," she thinks, for "any woman of modesty." Her cousin Maria does not share her concerns. Though already engaged, Maria happily flirts with Henry Crawford. Fanny flees his advances. To put it bluntly, Maria is fun. Fanny is boring.

Today we would say that Fanny has hang ups. She's embarrassed by attention and terrified by the prospect of intimacy. But maybe she's on to something. Maria flirts with Crawford and oversteps the bounds of discretion because she enjoys his attention and the thrill of pushing boundaries. She thinks she's in control of herself and the situation. She is wrong. She falls for Crawford and destroys her marriage. Fanny, on the other hand, who correctly estimates the power of romantic attractions and her own vulnerabilities, is able to guard her hopes and, ultimately, secure her happiness.

Here's another example. The first touchdown dance in NFL history was done in 1973 by Elmo Wright, a wide receiver for the Kansas City Chiefs. (He got into the end zone only six times in his career, so perhaps we should forgive his exuberance.) Since then the touchdown dance has become an elaborate ritual: the Ickey Shuffle, Merton Hanks's Chicken Dance, Jamal Anderson's Dirty Bird. Tim Tebow took a knee, Terrell Owens took a nap. My personal favorite was Barry Sanders's. When he scored a touchdown he would hand the ball to the official. He acted, in the words of Elmer Layden, like he had been there before.

It wasn't that he had an inferiority complex. He knew he was good. But he also put his accomplishments in proper perspective. Scoring a touchdown is impressive. But it's not brokering world peace. Reaching the end zone was Sanders's job, and he did it. "I tried to make sure I upheld my end," he said, "I took care of business and then I went home."

Here's a third example. General George McClellan used to call Abraham Lincoln a "well-meaning baboon." We think of Lincoln as Walt Whitman did—"O Captain! My Captain!" But in those days a number of people shared McClellan's opinion. Edwin Stanton called him a "long-armed ape." William Seward said he had "no conception of his situation [and] little application to great ideas."

Lincoln took it all with modesty. "It was better," he said, "at this time not to be making points of etiquette and personal dignity." He said he would cheerfully hold McClellan's horse if it would bring about victory.

Lincoln was no shrinking violet. He confessed to an ambition to be "esteemed of my fellow men." But he did not let his desire for esteem distort his judgment. He recognized the limits of his office and his own capabilities. And he knew he could realize his great ambition only with the support of others.

Fanny Price, Barry Sanders, Abraham Lincoln. Not three names you often hear in the same sentence. But all three epitomized the virtue of modesty. It's an admirable trait that moderates our actions and desires in accordance with an honest estimation of ourselves. Fanny, Barry, and Abe were able to estimate themselves honestly—their strength of character, the value of their deeds, the limits of their powers. That self-knowledge helped them secure their happiness and success.

When you practice modesty, you don't sell yourself short. Fanny exercised caution because she valued her own happiness and feelings. A touchdown doesn't require a chicken dance, because its value speaks for itself. Lincoln relied on others because he recognized the value of good counsel and the support of his friends.

How does a person practice modesty? First, you protect your virtues. All of them. Don't put yourself in situations that could lead you to vice. We were born to be saints, so we shouldn't settle for less. Second, you don't neglect your family and friends. You need their counsel, support, and prayers. Finally, you don't neglect your relationship with God. Pray every day. The greatest immodesty is to try to live without God. Without Him you can do nothing. With Him all things are possible.

STUDIOUSNESS

AQUINAS SAYS studiousness is an aspect of temperance. And it's not just a virtue for students. When we leave school we have new responsibilities: deadlines for work, phone calls to return, meetings to attend. These things are important. But they leave little time for reflection, contemplation, or sustained attention to any object of thought.

It's not only external events (meetings, phone calls) that distract us. Just as often the interruption comes from within. The poet Mary Oliver says we have "a self within the self that whistles and pounds upon the door panels and tosses itself, splashing, into the pond of meditation." It reminds you that "you must phone the dentist, that you are out of mustard, that your Uncle Stanley's birthday is two weeks hence."

The internet makes it particularly easy to distract ourselves. Think how many times a day you check your phone (Apple says 80 times a day, on average) or social media (Facebook says the average user spends 50 minutes a day on its site) or simply get lost browsing the web. You only intended to look up the date of the Gettysburg Address. An hour later you're reading about mutant super-viruses.

But I digress.

Studiousness is the virtue that moderates our natural desire to know, so we can devote attention to the right things in the right way.

This is important because there is, in fact, a right way to know things. We are inundated with information. We cram and consume it, we sell it, we use it to impress people at parties. It is easy to forget that there is a difference between information and knowledge, and that the difference consists in thinking about the information we have. The one-time Soviet spy Whittaker Chambers tells a story about watching his daughter sit in her highchair smearing porridge on her face. He came to believe in God while contemplating "the delicate convolutions of her ear." "Those intricate, perfect ears," Chambers thought, "could [only] have been created [by God's] design." (Chambers would have missed this moment if he had been scrolling through his news feed.)

The world is a gift from God. It takes its form

from his wisdom. Studiousness disposes us to know the world with wonder and gratitude. Ultimately it points us toward God.

This brings me to my second point. Studiousness is a virtue that prepares us for the spiritual life. There are times in life when it seems as if God is silent. Many great saints have experienced this sense of abandonment. St. Thérèse of Lisieux writes in her spiritual autobiography about the "thickest darkness" which God permitted to invade her soul.

But before we conclude that God is really being silent, we ought to ask ourselves whether we are really listening. When the Lord called to Samuel in a dream, Eli instructed him to say, "Speak, Lord, your servant is listening."

Prayer, the philosopher Simone Weil observed, "is the orientation of all the attention of which the soul is capable towards God." This is harder than it sounds. Often, we confuse attention "with a kind of muscular effort." We furrow our brows, purse our lips, hold our breath. This is not attention. True attention, Weil writes, "consists of suspending our thought, leaving it detached, empty and ready to be penetrated by the object."

Studiousness is the virtue of attention. It disposes us to want the truth, to seek it ardently, but also to wait attentively on it. When you practice studiousness in your daily life—when you read a book, look at a painting, talk to a friend—it prepares you to give your full attention to God. "If we concentrate our attention on trying to solve a problem of geometry," Weil observes, "and if at the end of an hour we are no nearer to doing so than at the beginning, we have nevertheless been making progress each minute of that hour in another more mysterious dimension.... It is certain that this effort will bear its fruit in prayer."

Allow me to offer some advice on cultivating the virtue of studiousness. First, don't confuse it with will power. Will power, Weil says, "has practically no place in study" because "the intelligence can only be led by desire .... The joy of learning is as indispensable in study as breathing is in running." As you enter the professional world, set aside time to become an amateur, that is, someone who pursues an action or thought, or cultivates a talent, for the love of it.

Second, devote your time and attention to things that deserve them. The natural world is a good place to start. Go outside and leave your cellphone inside.

Learn the names of the plants in your yard. Observe birds in flight and learn to distinguish their shapes and calls. "Attention," Mary Oliver says, "is the beginning of devotion."

Finally, set aside time every day to pray. Start small, just a few minutes, when you refuse all interruptions, put yourself in the presence of God, and say: "Speak, Lord, your servant is listening."

INDUSTRIOUSNESS

THE VIRTUE of industriousness is on Ben Franklin's list of 13 in his *Autobiography*. Here is what Franklin said about his effort at moral improvement:

It was about this time that I conceived the bold and arduous Project of arriving at moral Perfection. I wished to live without committing any Fault at any time; I would conquer all that either Natural Inclination, Custom, or Company might lead me into. As I knew, or thought I knew, what was right and wrong, I did not see why I might not always do the one and avoid the other. But I soon found I had undertaken a Task of more Difficulty than I had imagined. While my Attention was taken up in guarding against one Fault, I was often surprised by another. Habit took the Advantage of In-attention. Inclination was sometimes too strong for Reason. I concluded at length, that the mere speculative Conviction that it was our Interest to be completely virtuous, was not sufficient to prevent our Slipping, and that the contrary Habits must be broken and good ones acquired and established, before we can have any Dependence on a steady uniform Rectitude of Conduct. For this purpose I therefore contrived the following Method.

… I included under Thirteen Names of Virtues all that at that time occurred to me as necessary or desirable, and annexed to each a short Precept, which fully expressed the Extent I gave to its Meaning…. These Names of Virtues with their Precepts were …

6. Industry. Lose no Time. Be always employed in something useful. Cut off all unnecessary Actions.

There are many things in life you won't achieve unless you have learned the habit of industry. It's a good and useful quality of character. I have turned over in my own mind whether I would classify it as a virtue in the same league as the cardinal virtues and the theological virtues. It seems more … I don't know … American than those virtues. The very kind of thing you would expect the author of *Poor Richard's Almanac* to admire. It's almost capitalist. (Wasn't that Max Weber's point?)

As I have reflected on it, though, it has occurred to me that my suspicions of Franklin were a little unfair. The book of Proverbs praises this same virtue. A good wife, it says, "is far more precious than jewels."

She seeks wool and flax, and works with willing hands....
She rises while it is yet night and provides food for her
household and tasks for her maidens....
Her lamp does not go out at night.
She puts her hands to the distaff, and her hands hold the
spindle....
She ... does not eat the bread of idleness.

The difference, I have decided, is not in the effort but in the point of it. Franklin believed that "Early to bed, early to rise, makes a man healthy, wealthy and wise." Proverbs begins by saying "The fear of the Lord is the beginning of knowledge," and ends its praise of the good wife with the words "a woman who fears the Lord is to be praised."

The fear Proverbs is talking about is not like the fear of a tiger. It is the sense of awe we feel out of love for God. It is tied up with our adoration and reverence for him. We are called to the virtue that Franklin calls industry because the best we can do for our God is to use the gifts he has given us to their fullest extent. The gospel of Matthew makes the point unambiguously in the story of the master who went on a journey and entrusted his property to his servants—five to one, two to another, who both made good investments; one to a third, who buried it and was punished on the master's return.

Be sure you read all of Matthew 25. The parable is not saying (as Franklin might have done) that God is the ultimate capitalist and you are his broker, charged with getting him a good rate of return. It is immediately followed by the story of the last judgment, in which the sheep, placed at God's right hand, are those who fed the hungry, gave drink to the thirsty, welcomed the stranger, clothed the naked, visited the sick and the imprisoned. What we owe to God is to cultivate our talents for the service of others—in particular those in need.

MIDDLE AGE

A METAPHOR SUGGESTS that youth is the dawn of life and old age is its twilight. Middle age, then, is its midday. It's an illuminating comparison. The busiest part of life happens in middle age. There are many responsibilities and few reprieves. Some of life's newness has worn off, but rest seems far away and there is still much to do. The metaphor of an unrelenting midday sun is apt.

But middle age has another side. Dante, in fact, suggests it's the opposite of what we usually think, that it is more like a dark wood than a midday sun. He begins the *Divine Comedy*:

> At one point midway on our path in life,
> I came around and found myself now searching
> Through a dark wood, the right way blurred and lost.
> How hard it is to say what that world was,
> A wilderness, savage, brute, harsh and wild.
> Only to think of it renews my fear!

Carl Jung observed something similar about the challenges of middle age. But he saw a psychological crisis where Dante saw a spiritual one. Nevertheless, they shared a common observation. The middle of life is a time for taking an honest look at the path we are on and deciding whether or not to stay. Youth is full of choices. What should I study? What should I do for a living? Whom should I marry? It is the time for choosing a city, a political affiliation, a faith. In middle age, we revisit those choices. We ask: am I heading in the right direction? Am I happy with the life I have chosen? They can be unsettling questions. But they can also be fruitful. They may help us to correct course, as Dante did. They may force us to look for something deeper in life. They may also provide an opportunity to renew the commitments we've made.

Like youth, middle age has its own kind of beauty. It is a strenuous time of life. But it is filled with joy. Professional commitments seem unending, but work becomes easier with familiarity. The zeal and energy of youth may have worn off but in their place are knowledge and competence. A new kind of confidence arises, this time from experience rather than optimism.

Family life brings a different kind of rigor too, and a different kind of joy. Marriage feels different five, ten, or fifteen years in. People say that the excitement wears off. In a way, they are right. The demands of parenting are not easy. Toddlers are exhausting; teenagers are too. But raising children is fulfilling in a way that dating is not. There's nothing better in life than teaching your children about the solar system, or how to change a tire, or how to pray the rosary. You learn a lot along the way too. Married love blossoms into something even better than young love: mutual appreciation, respect, and admiration. With that comes the realization that you are building something much greater than you set out to.

Virtue steers the course through the challenges of middle age. It is what enables us to persevere in the commitments we've made. It is also what allows us to grow where we need to. Patience and constancy loom large. Truthfulness (with oneself and others) and meekness are often the keys to surviving the more difficult moments. Generosity and hospitality are fruits of having greater social responsibility and seeking to share the life you've built with others.

TRUTHFULNESS

IN THE *Nicomachean Ethics* Aristotle suggests that all virtues are means between vicious extremes. Truthfulness is the seventh virtue he mentions, of eleven moral virtues. Truth-telling, he says, is a mean between boasting (on the one hand), which involves exaggerating one's own qualities, and irony (on the other), which involves dismissing them. Exaggeration is the more serious vice. Even really virtuous people can occasionally be ironic and self-effacing. Think of Socrates, who claimed he knew nothing.

Aristotle has in mind the quality of being plain spoken in ordinary conversation. But I think he gets at a much deeper point. Untruthfulness subtracts from who we are because lies are small-minded. Emily Dickinson puts it this way:

> *A Counterfeit—a Plated Person—*
> *I would not be—*
> *Whatever strata of Iniquity*
> *My Nature underlie—*
> *Truth is good Health—and Safety, and the Sky.*
> *How meagre, what an Exile—is a Lie,*
> *And Vocal—when we die—*

Lies are "meagre." They always make us less than who we are, a counterfeit of ourselves. Augustine has a similar idea in *The City of God*. To lie is to live according to your own truth and not God's. In fact, that is what caused the devil to fall: "For the devil too wished to live according to himself when he did not abide in the truth ...."

The damage of a lie is perhaps never so acute as when we lie to ourselves. In *The Brothers Karamazov* Dostoyevsky writes:

Above all, don't lie to yourself. The man who lies to himself and listens to his own lie comes to such a pass that he cannot distinguish the truth within him, or around him, and so loses all respect for himself and others. And having no respect, he ceases to love.

It is no coincidence that many of our infamous criminals are pathological liars, as is the worst villain (and there are many) in *The Brothers Karamazov*. When the audience meets Smerdyakov, he is weaving a tangled web of facts and lies to cover up a murder. Smerdyakov tries to convince himself of his own innocence, and retreats further into evil and madness. But it need not be that dramatic. There is something about undermining the truth in casual situations that can eventually lead to the worst kind of spiritual death, the inability to love.

Augustine helps us understand this phenomenon. He writes, in *The Confessions*, "I have had experience with many who wished to deceive, but not one who wished to be deceived." If we strive to treat people as we wish to be treated, then we instinctively know that lying undermines our ability to love, because being lied to is hurtful. We only find ourselves in a sincere gift of self, the pastoral constitution *Gaudium et Spes* says. And that requires truthfulness. A lie withholds both the truth and ourselves.

So work on telling the truth. Make a habit of neither exaggerating nor understating your case. You will have deeper relationships, because people will trust you. Most importantly, you will become the kind of person who knows the truth, and is capable of love.

PATIENCE

IT'S AN OLD SAYING, "Patience is a virtue." But as virtues go, patience is not particularly heroic. It doesn't hold a candle to charity, which St. Paul says is the greatest of all virtues. It shines weakly beside the fortitude of Hector and the justice of Aristides. The benefits of patience are less visible than those of the other virtues. They accrue over time, through daily effort. "In patience you will possess your souls," Dorothy Day wrote. "Patience means suffering and suffering is spiritual work, and it is accomplishing something though we don't realize it until later."

Ted Williams was a patient hitter because he could take a few pitches to get one he liked. The same quality made him a great fisherman. Warren Buffett is a patient investor because he takes his time getting in and out of stocks. But true patience is about more than waiting for what you want. There's a moment in Tolkien's *The Fellowship of the Ring* when Gandalf has to choose from among the three routes through the mines of Moria. Hours go by and the party is stalled, but Gandalf takes his time with the decision. The mines are dangerous. The lives of his friends are at stake. But the mission is important. That's what makes it true patience. Patience waits for the right means to do what is good.

Gandalf was waiting on memory, instinct, and

prudence to tell him what to do. But often we are waiting on God. It's hard. St. Monica spent 17 years praying for the conversion of her son, St. Augustine. That's the spiritual work Dorothy Day was talking about. It might seem like fishing or waiting for a stock to pan out, but I think it's different. Patience is the disposition to wait for God's help. Monica was doing that. Ted Williams and Warren Buffett were not. Monica's persistence in knocking on God's door and waiting for an answer is what St. Paul meant when he said that "Love is patient ...." It's connected to faith and hope as well. Through faith we know God's promise of grace. Hope allows us to trust in that promise. Patience teaches us how to wait.

I remember twenty years after the fact one of my blunders as a father. When our daughter Becky was six she announced, one morning as I frantically bundled the kids up for school, that school had been cancelled that day. I was too experienced a parent to be taken in by so simple a trick. When she became insistent I gave her a swat and told her to saddle up and get in the car. Turned out, there was no school. She has not forgotten my failure to observe due process. Nor have I. The lesson I learned that day was, hear people out. Even if you're sure you're right. Even if they're six. They may have a point. God may be working in what they say. Patience is the seedbed of humility, and justice.

It's not just a virtue we employ in dealing with children and spouses. When I was 16 I went to nerd camp at Cornell to study math. I was from a small town, and the other kids were from Boston and New York City. It was the first time I'd ever met anybody who was smart. I struggled to understand Riemann sums in a class of students who had 800's on their SATs. I would pound my pillow in frustration at night. I didn't go as far as Ajax and impale myself on my own slide rule. But acting on some juvenile death wish, I started smoking cigarettes. It took me several years to learn patience with my own human failings—and the more important lesson that God had a good plan for me, and it didn't involve approximating the area underneath a curve. Patience is the ground that hope grows in. The Koran tells us, "O you who believe, seek assistance through patience and prayer; surely Allah is with the patient."

Life is filled with uncertainties—many practical questions about what we should do, and whom we should do it with—that we need to figure out. It's important to have the patience to answer these questions right. And to do so we need to get up every morning with the disposition to await God's grace.

GENEROSITY

COMMENCEMENT speakers customarily exhort their audiences to use their degrees to "give back." The unstated premise of this appeal is that society has given young graduates a host of privileges—time, money, education, connections—and justice requires them to repay the favor by making a commensurate contribution.

It's not a bad argument. Justice is a cardinal virtue, and it's one I am particularly attached to, as a lawyer. The exhortation to give back implies that we have a duty to even out the distribution of social goods. In the same way, we might talk about "returning a favor." But generosity is not about balancing accounts. As Pope Francis has said, it "can transcend and overflow the demands of justice, 'expecting nothing in return[.]'"

A few years ago there was a fad at Starbucks drive-thrus, probably started by a sappy Helen Hunt/Kevin Spacey film called *Pay It Forward*. I pull up and pay for my medium latte, and tell the barista that I'd like to pay for the guy in the car behind me. Nice. But then of course it becomes a thing, and the guy behind me feels like he has to pay for the next person in line. And so on. Starbucks employees get into the act and ask if you too would like to pay it forward. In 2014 a drive-thru in St. Petersburg, Florida had a pay-it-forward chain going for 457 customers when Peter Schorsch broke ranks.

Paying it forward is not generosity either. The practice imposes a social obligation to keep replenishing the escrow account. There may be a kind of justice in this. After all, you have benefited from it. (Though as Mr. Schorsch pointed out, he got a $6 venti mocha frappuccino and someone down the line might order a $2 black coffee. "This is unfair to that person who paid for me.")

In the early months of the Covid-19 pandemic, NBC Nightly News ran a story about how Tyler Perry picked up the tab for senior citizens at more than 70 grocery stores in Georgia and Louisiana. The beneficiaries of Tyler Perry's generosity, shoppers at

Winn-Dixie, got a piece of paper that read "random act of kindness." That phrase is a little older than "pay it forward." It comes from a 1993 book by Anne Herbert, *Random Kindness & Senseless Acts of Beauty*. It's a little closer to the virtue I'm promoting, but still wide of the mark.

If our generosity really is random, it will miss the people who are the natural objects of our bounty. We'll end up buying a caramel macchiato for a guy in a BMW, rather than helping the man selling pencils at a subway entrance. Tyler Perry's act wasn't random. It helped old people who needed groceries. Mr. Schorsch, who broke the Starbucks pay-it-forward chain, was also generous rather than random. He tipped the barista $100. "I'm not trying to be a Grinch," he said. "I know things are hard for baristas and I am willing to help people."

Doing random acts of kindness is a prescription for a world without meaning. It's not clear why, other than for aesthetic reasons, we should commit ourselves to that course rather than to random acts of violence and senseless acts of cruelty. But that's not the world we live in. The gospel message is that God is love, and that creation, incarnation, and redemption were acts of the utmost generosity. God did not create the world, as England conquered India, in a fit of absent-mindedness. He did it to share his love with us. When we spurned his love he came into the world to show us by example how he wants us to love each other.

True generosity is guided by love, and love is never random. Charles Dickens understood why. After Ebenezer Scrooge was visited by the three ghosts of Christmas, he did not dedicate himself to random acts of kindness. Such a transformation would have been incomplete. Instead, Scrooge sought to use his wealth to care for those in his immediate circle, the people he'd inflicted his cruelty upon every day, like Bob Cratchit. His generosity was about them, and not about him. It turned his attention from his own good to the good of another. That's true generosity.

That's my recommendation. Don't limit your ambitions to giving back, returning favors, and paying it forward. These are nice things to do, but they are not truly generous. Practice true generosity. You'll know it by its connection to love.

MEEKNESS

AT THE Art Institute of Chicago there is a 17th century French painting of a woman feeding a lamb. It's by Eustache Le Sueur, one of the founders of the Royal Academy of Painting and Sculpture. You can see it in the Art Institute's online gallery. It shows a woman patting a lamb. Her face is serene. So is the lamb's. She wears a gold robe that complements Le Sueur's gold background. The colors and figures are all in harmony. Le Sueur made it for an altarpiece honoring the Virgin Mary. The painting is entitled *Meekness*.

The painting gets at something important about the virtue it represents. Meekness is certainly related to serenity. The meek shall "delight in abundance of peace," Psalm 36 says. They shall "inherit the earth," according to the Sermon on the Mount. St. Augustine says the meek have a special kind of stability: they draw their peace from God, and nothing can rob them of that.

But there's something missing too. Meekness is not as mellow as the painting suggests. Aquinas says it's the virtue that restrains anger and bestows self-possession. It quiets wrath and the urge to vengeance. It is not, as Nietzsche thought, a false virtue that turns weakness into an accomplishment. Quite the opposite. It requires strength. It forces you to get over yourself. The meek find peace and serenity (Le Sueur gets that right) but it takes hard work to get there. Anger is a strong and violent foe.

Anger is not a bad thing in itself. It's often understandable, even justified. But it's a passion you can lose control of. That's why we call rage "blind." The problem with anger, Aquinas says, is that it presents "a very great obstacle to man's free judgment of truth." It can render us susceptible to deception and incapable of sound judgment.

Shakespeare captures the fatal aspect of anger in *The Tragedy of Othello*. Things end badly for Othello and his wife Desdemona, you may recall. He comes to believe she has been unfaithful, and kills her. The tragedy is that it comes to this. The play begins with their declarations of love.

The villain of the play, Iago, plants seeds of doubt; but Othello's anger does the rest. Seeing Desdemona's handkerchief in the hands of another man pushes him over the edge. Othello no longer sees her goodness and fidelity. He forgets what she gave up for love of him. Iago is a master deceiver; of all Shakespeare's villains, he may be the worst. Othello's anger leads him to miss that too. As Aquinas says, it presents "a very great obstacle to [his] free judgment of truth." Meekness is the virtue he needed.

For Othello the lack of meekness was tragic. For Desdemona it was deadly. For us the stakes may be lower. Still, the example is instructive. Meekness will matter in our friendships. It doesn't mean abandoning our principles. But it will help us make reasoned arguments when things really matter. It will keep our friendships intact when opinions diverge. We will probably learn something. We will grow in wisdom. And we'll keep our friends.

Meekness matters equally on the job. At times your work won't meet with the approval of your boss or a colleague. It's natural then to get angry, but that's the wrong reaction. The virtue of meekness helps you take criticism constructively. It will make you a better employee, and eventually, a better boss.

Most of all, it matters in marriage. You need to listen with an open mind to what your spouse has to say. If you approach it with meekness, marriage is a sacrament of growth. It doesn't mean you become a doormat. But meekness helps keep anger at bay and accept the truth of what your spouse has to say.

Meekness confers the kind of serenity Le Sueur had in mind. But it takes hard work and grace to get there. It's worth the effort.

CONSTANCY

ST. VENANTIUS is a lesser-known saint who was martyred in the year 250 at the age of 15. When he learned he was about to be arrested Venantius turned himself in to Antiochus, the governor of Camerino, and began preaching to him. *Butler's Lives* tells us that "[w]hen it was found impossible to shake his constancy either by threats or promises, he was condemned to be scourged, but was miraculously saved by an Angel."

For several days after that Venantius was treated like some character in a bad Steven Seagal movie (*Hard to Kill*). His persecutors tried every way they could to kill him. They burned him with torches, then suspended him over a low fire so the smoke would suffocate him. An angel stamped out the fire. They threw him to the lions, but the lions crouched at his feet. They threw him over a cliff. They broke his teeth, dragged him through thorns, put him in a furnace. Angels rescued him each time. Eventually the governor threw in the towel and had him decapitated.

Venantius exhibited in extreme form the virtue of constancy. It is a graduation virtue. We pledge it in yearbooks: "Best friends forever." (Or my personal favorite, "Stay the way you are and you'll never change.") The Beach Boys adjure us to "Be true to your school."

Part of the explanation for that is nostalgia, a reluctance to let go. Aquinas observes that "[o]ne is said to be constant because one stands to a thing." But what is so praiseworthy about standing still? Especially for younger people, perched on the verge of their careers, with higher ambitions—to be a doctor; to land on the moon; to cure cancer; to be president. These dreams seem inconsistent with a virtue whose distinguishing feature is unchangeability.

But I'm not sure they are, if we envision the right kind of stillness. Think of a compass. The thing about a magnetized needle is that it never moves, no matter your weather or position. It doesn't get distracted by passing attractions.

This surprising steadiness would be interesting,

if that were all. What makes it a big deal is that the needle always points north. The virtue of constancy has this quality too. It points in a particular direction, a kind of true north outside our control. Constant attention to taste or fashion is not a virtue, only a hobby. Constant preoccupation with drugs is a vice. The virtue of constancy points us in another direction.

There is a wonderful little poem by George Herbert that makes the point. Herbert was a friend of Francis Bacon. His mother was a patron of John Donne, the metaphysical poet he closely resembles. Herbert gave up being Public Orator at Cambridge to live the simple life of an Anglican rector in a small village near Salisbury. Apart from tending his flock he preached and wrote poetry. One poem, for the second Sunday of Lent, is entitled *Constancy*. It begins:

> *Who is the honest man?*
> *He that does still and strongly good pursue,*
> *To God, his neighbor, and himself most true:*
> *Whom neither force nor fawning can*
> *Unpin, or wrench from giving all their due.*

The virtue of constancy points still and strongly toward the good. It directs us to be true to God, our neighbors, and ourselves.

Think about the biggest commitments we make in life. The faith described in Deuteronomy is a rule of constant attention: "I am the Lord your God .... You shall have no other gods before me." Marriage vows are a promise of constancy: to have and to hold, from this day forward, for better, for worse, for richer, for poorer, in sickness and in health, till death do us part. A lawyer admitted to the bar takes a vow: to "bear true faith and allegiance to the Commonwealth of Massachusetts ...." The Florence Nightingale Pledge is also one: "I solemnly pledge myself before God ... to pass my life in integrity and to practice my profession faithfully."

None of this is inconsistent with running for president, say, but it does mean that getting elected is not itself our true north. We should aim instead at the good we can do, and if that takes us to the Oval Office, so be it. Herbert says of the constant man that he

> *... when great trials come,*
> *Nor seeks, nor shuns them; but does calmly stay,*

Till he the thing and the example weigh:
All being brought into a sum,
What place or person calls for, he does pay.

My father was a small town lawyer who never left home except to attend school and fight the war. He had many admirable qualities, and among them was a trait his children came to know him for: you always knew exactly where he stood on life's important issues. He would calmly stay when great trials came. After a while you didn't even have to ask for his advice. You knew he would be pointing north, and you knew where that was.

That is something we should strive for, to be someone about whom our spouse and children and friends are able to say: "He was someone I could depend on." Be constant. Be true to God, your neighbor, and yourself.

HOSPITALITY

VICTOR HUGO once claimed that the third book of Dante's *Divine Comedy*, the Paradiso, was a little dull. "When the poem becomes happy it becomes boring," he said. I like the Paradiso, but Hugo has a point. Depicting heaven is notoriously difficult, even for the most talented artists and poets. The most sublime visions leave us a little unsatisfied. Maybe that is the point. Art and poetry can only do so much.

When Jesus spoke of heaven he often compared it to a feast. "The kingdom of heaven is like a king who prepared a wedding banquet for his son" he says in Matthew (Matthew 22). In Luke he speaks of "confer[ring] a kingdom ... so that you may eat and drink at my table in my kingdom and sit on thronesb ..." (Luke 22). In the Gospel of John, Jesus prepares rooms for those he loves: "And when I go and prepare a place for you, I will come again and will take you to myself, that where I am you may be also" (John 14). Those who were prepared enter a great wedding feast in the parable of the virgins (Matthew 25).

We know from the wedding feast at Cana that Jesus liked a good party. But I think this metaphor for heaven is about more than that. It has something to do with the meaning of hospitality. When we are children, we tend to think of heaven in terms of what's in it for us. Will heaven have video games? Will you have to do homework? Will my dog be there? Will there be ice cream? Jesus's images of a feast capture something of that. A good feast meets (and surpasses) our wants and needs. There's something in it for everyone. But something else happens at a feast too. Our wants and needs are satisfied so that we might focus our attention on other people. A feast is mostly about losing ourselves in the joy of giving our attention to others. Love is by its nature social, Fulton Sheen says. "Its greatest happiness is to gird its loins and serve the banquet of life."

Hospitality is the virtue that creates the circumstances for the social dimension of love to flourish. We are promised perfect hospitality in heaven. Here on earth, we have a foretaste of it in the Church. Catholics are welcomed every hour of every day at masses in churches across the globe. Anyone, wherever he's from, however much money he has, the language he speaks, or the burdens he carries, is encouraged to come and worship.

We experience a foretaste of heaven through our hospitality toward one another too. When we receive another into our home as though he were Christ, as St. Benedict instructs us to do, we make space for friendship. We also make space for joy. This goes for welcoming strangers as well as friends. St. Paul urges the Hebrews, "Be not forgetful to entertain strangers: for thereby some have entertained angels unawares" (Hebrews 13:2). St. Paul is not saying that you should invite just anyone into your home. That would be imprudent. And it misses the real point. We should invite those with whom we don't normally associate, even those we expect we might not enjoy. They might surprise us. More than that, they will remind us that every act of hospitality may be blessed.

Emily Dickinson reminds us that in heaven it will be that way:

> "Remember me" implored the Thief!
> Oh Hospitality!
> My Guest "Today in Paradise"
> I give thee guaranty.

A common criminal is not one whom we expect to be Jesus's honored guest at the heavenly feast. But the good thief had room in his heart to be loved; "remember me" he said to Jesus. That's all Jesus needed of him. It's all he needs of us too. G.K. Chesterton once asked, "How much bigger would your life be if your self could be smaller in it?" Making room for love makes our lives bigger and our selves smaller. And that's where hospitality begins.

OLD AGE

A NUMBER OF YEARS AGO the authors of the President's Council on Bioethics report on aging observed a paradox about old age in the modern world.[1] Today we spend more of our lives in youth than ever before. We also spend more time in decline. We are young for longer and we are aged for longer. Old age is no longer a stage of life only enjoyed by a few, and briefly. Rather, it has become an integral part of human experience.

The poet Matthew Arnold makes it sound no fun at all. He writes in "Growing Old":

> *It is to spend long days*
> *And not once feel that we were ever young;*
> *It is to add, immured*
> *In the hot prison of the present, month*
> *To month with weary pain.*

1. The President's Council on Bioethics "Taking Care: Ethical Caregiving in Our Aging Society." Available at https://bioethicsarchive .georgetown.edu/pcbe/reports/taking_care/index.html

The President's Council is less cynical. It's true enough that aging takes a toll on the body, and that physical limitations are a drag. But that is only one piece of aging. Grandparents often say that being a grandparent has all the fun of parenthood but little of its responsibility. Grandmothers can offer cookies without worrying about the kids' teeth. A grandfather can keep the children up past their bedtime but he doesn't have to hear complaints when they have to wake up for school tomorrow. Aging releases us from other responsibilities as well. Many people retire. Some replace work with hobbies and interests. Others travel. Don't like the winter climate? You can spend the winter on the beach in Florida.

Old age has its own purposes as well. It is a time for reflection. You have as much experience as a human being can while on earth. If you've lived well, you probably have a lot of wisdom too. There's joy in reflecting on life from that vantage point. Old age is a time to enjoy more fully family and friends. It is a gift to be able to watch your adult children parent their own offspring, and a blessing to see what sort of people they have become.

Late in life we make a different but important contribution to the common good as well. The ethicist William F. May has written about the effect of an aging population on younger people. The observation of virtue in the aging "can instruct and sometimes even inspire. Their example can encourage particularly the fainthearted among the young who believe that full human existence is possible only under the accidental circumstances of their own temporary flourishing." Their virtue reminds young people that goodness is a lifelong project. It is easier to be patient in the middle of life, when a noisy child is less bothersome. But it is more heroic to be patient in old age. It is easier to be courageous in your twenties, when death still seems far off. It's heroic to be courageous in old age, when death is nearer.

Like the other stages of life, old age requires many of the virtues that are common to all. But specific virtues tend to be of additional importance. Repentance and mercy dispose us rightly toward past injustices. Gratitude allows us to receive help graciously. Gentleness and benignity are the fruits of having lived a lot of life. Magnanimity allows us to use the resources we have accumulated over a lifetime in the service of others.

REPENTANCE

REPENTANCE, unlike mercy, is not a divine attribute. It's a virtue for sinners and stumblers. Maybe that's why we're so bad at it. On the campaign trail Donald Trump once put it this way: "I think apologizing is a great thing, but you have to be wrong."

St. Thomas says that the virtue of repentance has three effects: sorrow, confession, and satisfaction. It's the second part we struggle with. We don't like to say we're sorry.

We say "Sorry but ...." This is what the lawyers call confession and avoidance. Adam admitted he ate the apple. But, he said, "It was the woman you gave me who gave me the fruit." Like it was Eve's fault. Or God's! We say "Sorry if I offended you." This is the jiu-jitsu apology. It cleverly shifts the weight of blame. It wasn't my failing, but your thin skin or wrong-headedness. The extreme form of this is what William Schneider calls the past exonerative tense. It takes the penitent entirely out of the picture. "Mistakes were made," Ronald Reagan famously said, about the arms-for-hostages deal with Iran.

Most often we don't apologize at all. We wait for

things to blow over. Or, feeling contrite but reluctant to go the whole hog, we make amends without an apology. Agamemnon did this in the *Iliad*, after taking Briseis from Achilles. To appease Achilles's wrath he offered to return her along with vast wealth. But as Maimonides observes, "Someone who injures a colleague or damages his property does not attain atonement, even though he pays him what he owes, until he confesses."

A good apology follows a simple formula: name the offense, say you're sorry, ask forgiveness. In *The Wind in the Willows* Mole tips over Rat's boat after ignoring Rat's instruction. The miserable and wet Mole then says: "Ratty, my generous friend! I am very sorry indeed for my foolish and ungrateful conduct .... Indeed, I have been a complete ass, and I know it. Will you overlook this once and forgive me, and let things go on as before?" The effect is remarkable. Rat replies at once: "That's all right, bless you!" And they go on, closer friends than before.

Repent! It comes across as a strange message today. You'd expect to see it on a sign in Lafayette Park: The end is near! But repentance is serious business. I have been married for the better part of five decades and I have five children, all now grown up. I have had a lot of opportunities to apologize. I have learned that repentance is the duct tape of family life. It can fix anything. "The right words, spoken at the right time," Pope Francis said, "daily protect and nurture love." I promise you. Life will be happier if you cultivate the virtue of repentance. This sounds counterintuitive. We think of penitents wearing sackcloth and ashes. But when you apologize, you open the door for mercy. And mercy brings peace. Those are the words of absolution: "May God grant you his pardon and peace."

So make a practice of apologizing. Make confession a part of your routine. We all need to receive God's mercy.

GRATITUDE

A RECENT ANNOUNCEMENT by the National Center for Health Statistics observed that the number of babies born in the U.S. in 2020 was down 4% from 2019. This was the sixth consecutive year the number of births declined. America's overall fertility rate is now at 1.64, the lowest level since we began keeping track a century ago, and well below replacement rate (2.1).

This got me thinking it's a lucky thing our parents didn't take such a dim view of reproduction. If the fertility rate had been 1.64 at the turn of the century, 21% of the average college graduation class wouldn't be around to march. It also got me thinking about gratitude, an appropriate virtue for occasions like commencements.

Gratitude is not just an emotion. We are always grateful *for* something—a sunny day, a loving family, an education. But in every case we are grateful *to* someone—to God, our parents, our benefactors. This is well expressed in the doxology we sing to the tune of *Old 100th:* "Praise God from whom all blessings flow; Praise Him all creatures here below[.]" Or in the song *I Love My Momma* by Snoop Dogg: "I just want to say I love you for life/ and that's the reason why I'm here now/ Love Snoop."

Here's another interesting thing. Gratitude is due only for things that are freely given to us. I have reached the point in life where I am eligible for Medicare. People can get Medicare Part A (hospital insurance) if they are 65 years old and have paid Medicare taxes for 10 years. If I were hospitalized for Covid I would expect the government to pay, but I wouldn't be grateful. I've paid Medicare tax (1.45% with no cap) most of my life and I figure the government owes me.

In fact, in languages derived from Latin we use the same word (*grace*, from *gratia*) to denote both the favor freely given and our thankfulness for it. Theologians use *grace* to refer to the unmerited influence of divine love operating in us for our sanctification. Thus the Council of Trent maintained that the sacraments confer grace *ex opere operato*—as God's gift, and not because of the work of the minister or the faith of the recipient.

And by extension, since granting favors is the preserve of the great and the good, the English use "your Grace" as a style of address for dukes and archbishops. Thus Wilton Gregory, the Cardinal Archbishop of Washington, would be "his Grace" as well as "his Eminence."

At the same time, when we speak of *grace* before and after meals, we have in mind our thankfulness for what has been given to us: "Bless us, O Lord, and these Thy gifts which we are about to receive from Thy bounty ...." And "We give Thee thanks, O Lord, for these and all Thy benefits which we have received from Thy goodness ...."

So one expresses gratitude to some other person for gifts freely given. This describes well the debt we owe our parents. Their bringing us into the world was the freest sort of creative act. Their effort to feed, clothe, house, and educate us was a work they undertook simply because they loved us.

There is a danger that attends this relationship. The one who receives is in an inferior position. His weakness or dependence might cause him to feel resentment, and the giver to nourish a sense of power or superiority.

Parents learn this lesson when their children go off to college. The love that brought their offspring into the world, the love that raised and supported them and helped them get a university education, should not demand repayment or it is not deserving of gratitude. Romano Guardini said that "he who gives must do so with reverence for the one who receives; otherwise, he wounds the receiver's self-respect."

And here is one last thing about gratitude. Aquinas says that one who confers a benefit gives two things: the affection of the heart and the gift. So too with one who receives. He should return the affection immediately. But he should also return the favor itself, in greater measure if possible, and at a time when it will serve the benefactor. True gratitude moves us to practice the generosity we ourselves benefit from.

The ancients agree, though, that there is one particular case where we may be unable to make an adequate return. St. Thomas, citing both Aristotle and Seneca, says "it is not possible to make ... equal repayment to ... one's parents." Were it not for them, we would have no diploma ceremonies, because we would have no students.

MERCY

ST. THOMAS asks whether mercy might actually be the greatest of the virtues. He decides in the end that it is not, but it's up there.

Older people will recall the attempt made on the life of Pope John Paul II on May 13, 1981. Four bullets hit him and he nearly died of blood loss. In the days afterward the pope asked people to pray for the man who shot him. He offered words of forgiveness even before he'd left his hospital bed. Two years later he met privately with the shooter, who was then in jail.

The photographs of that meeting were widely aired in the media.

There was something powerful about that simple act. It captured the attention of Christians and non-Christians alike. It was persuasive. John Paul II did some magnificent things in his life. He changed the map of Europe. He wrote brilliant theology. He inspired the youth of the Church. But of all these things, I think he might be most remembered for this act of mercy.

Mercy is a tricky virtue. It is related to justice. But justice is much easier to understand, because everyone gets his due. We Christians know that justice isn't the complete story. We are grateful it's not, because we are sinners, and sinners (forgive the old-fashioned and judgmental language) deserve hell. If we are bound for heaven (and we hope we are), it's because of God's mercy.

In *The Merchant of Venice* Portia puts it this way:

Though justice be thy plea, consider this,
That in the course of justice none of us
Should see salvation: we do pray for mercy;
And that same prayer doth teach us all to render
The deeds of mercy.

Mercy is a gift. First and foremost, it's a gift we receive from God. It's not something we can pay back. (That would be justice.) As one of Graham Greene's characters says: "You can't conceive, my child, nor can I or anyone—the ... appalling ... strangeness of the mercy of God."

When we show mercy to one another, we do it in imitation of Christ. "Love one another as I have loved you" and "be merciful, just as your Father is merciful" were Jesus's instructions to the disciples. When the scribes and Pharisees sought to punish a woman caught in adultery, Jesus responded "Let the one among you who is without sin be the first to throw a stone at her."

The virtues always say something about who we are. The cardinal virtues speak to the goodness of human nature. The theological virtues speak to our heavenly end. The virtue of mercy shows that we have received a gift. It tells the story of our salvation, the history of our lives as Christians.

Young people tend to take their responsibilities seriously. They respect confidentiality better than older people often do. When they serve on disciplinary boards, they are stricter than their elders. They are uncompromising in their judgments, of movies, food, public figures, parents. We can admire their integrity. It is part of the idealism that makes it a joy to live and work with them.

Mercy is foreign to the idealist's nature. It is a grandparent's virtue. Unlike justice it doesn't follow rules. If we replaced punishment with mercy, we would have anarchy. Article II of the Constitution entrusts mercy to the President's unreviewable discretion because in public life there is no rule for applying it.

But in the love of two people it is essential. There there is no room for just deserts. We must make it a rule always to give and forgive. In our friendships too, we should replace judgment with mercy. And if we practice this virtue in our inner circles, it will soften the sharp edges of our ideals just enough, and make us much more effective leaders, lieutenants, teachers, doctors, architects, or conductors.

MAGNANIMITY

VICTOR HUGO'S *Les Misérables* is one of the great works of French literature. Jean Valjean, its protagonist, is the best of Hugo's characters. He is a convict (he stole a loaf of bread to feed a child). We meet him when he's just finished serving a nineteen-year sentence. *Les Misérables* follows Valjean's life after prison. He becomes a wealthy and successful businessman. He's known for his generosity and justness. When an innocent woman accused of misconduct is fired from one of his businesses and later dies, he adopts her child as his own. Later, given the opportunity to exact vengeance on his nemesis, Valjean opts for mercy.

What attracts us to Jean Valjean is his greatness of soul, or magnanimity. Aristotle describes this as the virtue concerned with great things. The magnanimous man, the philosopher says (he was a little less evolved than we are; this goes equally for women), is one who thinks he is capable of great things and worthy of honor—and he's right. A person who overestimates his merit is a fool. And one who underestimates himself is unduly humble.

But those who are magnanimous, Aristotle continues, disdain goods like wealth and power. It helps if they have them, because people with wealth and power are in a better position to confer benefits on others. Magnanimous people like to help others, but don't like to ask for help. Magnanimous people think they are superior to other people, but still treat them with courtesy. And magnanimous people characteristically don't involve themselves in petty tasks. You wouldn't see them taking out the trash or doing laundry. They're only interested in great and noble tasks. They lead armies, run countries, found charities.

From Aristotle's account, magnanimity might sound more like the vice of pride than like a virtue. We know Jesus told his disciples that "whoever would be great among you must be your servant, and whoever would be first among you must be a slave of all." And if magnanimity is a virtue, it might not seem particularly well suited to most of us. Most of us don't have great fortunes that we can give away. We generally need to rely on the help of others as we make our way in the world. And plenty of us have to take out the trash and do our own laundry.

I do think Aristotle was on to something, though I don't think he had the complete picture. It's a virtue to recognize your own greatness and to act accordingly, provided you know where that greatness comes from and what it really consists in. Perhaps that's why I prefer Hugo's version. At the beginning of *Les Misérables* Valjean steals a basket of silverware from

Bishop Myriel, a kind clergyman who has offered him help. He's caught in the act by police. On learning of his arrest, Myriel declares that he has done no wrong. The silverware was a gift, he says. The man's only fault was having forgotten the valuable candlesticks he offered with it.

The scene is famous for good reason. The fate of Valjean's soul hinges on Myriel's generosity. Aristotle would have been surprised to find magnanimity in an ex-con. But Hugo wasn't. What the latter perceives is that magnanimity has its true source in God. Following this act of mercy, the bishop tells Valjean:

My brother, you no longer belong to evil, but to good. It is your soul that I buy from you; I withdraw it from black thoughts and the spirit of perdition, and I give it to God.

Valjean never forgets this lesson. He knows his greatness comes to him as a gift. Were it not for the bishop he would have been a prisoner for life. The wealth and power he later acquires become a means of doing good for others.

True magnanimity is always accompanied by humility. "Magnanimity," Aquinas says, "makes a man deem himself worthy of great things in consideration of the gifts he holds from God." Humility recalls our limitations as fallen creatures; magnanimity recalls the greatness of which we are capable when we rely on God. In both cases, we recall who we are in God's eyes, our dependence upon him. God created us in his image and likeness and has called us to share in his divine life. We were made to become saints. We do so only with God's help. This is the real greatness of human nature, and the grandeur of the human vocation.

It's a daunting task, and it's tempting to shrink away from it. Magnanimity is the virtue that disposes us to accept the greatness of our nature and strive to live accordingly.

Let me offer three pieces of advice:

First, you may not have the financial wealth to found a charity or endow a scholarship. You have, though, received many gifts: your intellect, your education, most important, your faith. These are treasures. Use them well and share them with others.

Second, Aristotle was right about treating all people with courtesy. But he was wrong about the looking down on them part. Every person you meet is a child of God. They deserve your respect.

Finally, your job and the chores of daily life may not seem like great and noble tasks. But great and noble accomplishments begin with small steps done well. Before Mother Teresa founded her first home for the dying, she picked up one sick woman on the street and carried her to a hospital. Mother Teresa wasn't born Mother Teresa. She became a great saint because she made little choices every day. One of her favorite sayings was: "Do small things with great love." The great task of your life is to become a saint. You can begin today by doing even the most menial tasks with love.

GENTLENESS

GENTLENESS is an underappreciated virtue that is practiced too little in the world. These days we employ social media to debate issues of public importance, and too often, to make personal attacks on people whose views differ from our own. In the worst cases, those who hold the wrong ideas are punished, or even "cancelled." Think of James Bennet, an opinion editor at the New York Times who lost his job over running an unpopular opinion piece. Or of Matt Yglesias, a columnist at Vox (a publication he co-founded)

who departed the publication after blowback for crit-
icizing the term "Latinx." Some people claim this is a
matter of holding people accountable for their ideas.
But often these reactions set aside ideas and arguments. They're not about changing minds. They're
about penalizing people for holding views we don't
like.

What is needed here is greater charity. Charity is
the virtue that allows us to love the one with whom
we disagree. Along the way we need the help of another virtue: gentleness. Aristotle says the virtue of gentleness is the mean with respect to anger. The gentle
person "is angry at the right things and with the right
people." And he "errs in the direction of deficiency."
He makes allowances for others' flaws rather than fly-
ing off the handle.

Meekness has a similar job. In fact, gentleness and
meekness are often treated as interchangeable. Some
translations of the Sermon on the Mount say it is the
meek who inherit the earth. Others say it is the gentle.
Both virtues tell us how to manage our anger. Both
help us to avoid rage or wrath. But meekness seems
to be interior, while gentleness addresses how we act.
The meek person maintains an interior serenity that

allows him to manage his anger. The gentle person acts with kindness and generosity toward those who have been the cause of his anger. The meek receive criticism well; the gentle give it well.

That's the part I want to emphasize. Because it has never been easier to express outrage, out loud and in public. Twenty, even ten years ago, you could express anger by writing an op-ed or a letter to the editor. You could call your senator or start a letter campaign. All these things took time, and time forced you to weigh your response and allowed your anger to cool. Today those checks are gone. We can instantly take a side on any issue. We can condemn people we have never met for a misstep or a tasteless joke. We can do it in real time in 280 characters.

The trouble is, these knee-jerk reactions are usually overblown. The world is not populated by Lord Voldemorts, characters evil to the core. It is filled with people. Many (heck, all) are sinful and flawed, but God loved them enough to give his life for them. If God shows them mercy, who are we to condemn them without qualification?

The virtue of gentleness helps us put the brakes on anger. It allows us to see offenses in perspective, and offenders as people whom God loves. Jesus said the gentle are blessed because they will inherit the earth. That seems counterintuitive. It seems more likely that Vladimir Putin and ISIS will inherit the earth, and that nice guys will finish last.

But the meaning of the beatitude is that gentleness brings peace. And anger will destroy our peace. We describe angry people, with good reason, as "consumed with rage" or "seeing red." Anger distorts us and our perception of reality. When we are mastered by anger, it taints every pleasure, and makes it hard to see anything but that which offends. Be gentle. "Do not let the sun go down on your anger." Because it gives the devil an opportunity to steal your peace.

St. Paul, in his letter to the Galatians, also lists gentleness among the fruits of the Holy Spirit. This means it's a trait we acquire with the Holy Spirit's assistance. So if you are lacking in gentleness, pray for it.

BENIGNITY

BENIGNITY is a virtue I have come to admire in old people. My grandfather, who lived to be 95, had it in abundance. You could tell him anything—your most embarrassing faults—and he could see past them to the person you aspired to be. He never lost sight of your good qualities. People loved to sit with him for this reason. With a smile and a look in his eye he communicated to you the feeling that you were the most interesting ... the smartest, funniest, most admirable person he had ever met.

I thought I had him fooled. It was hard to get that kind of affirmation from other people because they could see through me. But Grandfather took me at face value. I thought.

In the last decade I have come to understand that he looked right through me and still loved what he saw. This is the virtue I have in mind. The old writers called it benignity. Francis Arias, S.J., a Spaniard received into the Society of Jesus three years after St. Ignatius died, wrote a treatise on the subject. Here is how he described it:

There are men, who in very truth have the essential part of the virtue of charity with their neighbors, both friends & enemies; both wishing them good and performing it to them: but yet they ... are austere and sharp in their conversation, and dry and untoward in performing the very good, which they do.

The virtue of Benignity, doth cure and heal a man of all these defects.

In more modern language we would call it kindness, as the prophet Micah does. It is not charity, but the way we perform it.

It's fair to say benignity is a second-string virtue. It's not up there with the big guys—faith, hope, charity, justice, fortitude. And yet it is still a virtue that we do well to cultivate. A person may be good at making clear and correct judgments, about what acts are right, good, and just, and what are their opposites. But that is not enough. We must guard against extending this habit from acts to people. Certainly none of us is an angel. And most of us deal on a regular basis with people who do bad things. But in most cases that is not all they are. We should try always to look right through them and still love them for what they are.

Remember this modest lesson when you are tempted to make a sharp reply or a harsh judgment. If you can cultivate this homely little virtue, you will soon be the sort of person everyone wants to be around.

THE CROWN OF
VIRTUES

THERE'S NOW A VOGUE in home renovation
shows. Bob Vila and *This Old House* used to be
the only option. Now whole networks are dedicated
to home renovation programming. Chip and Joanna
Gaines started a show about fixing up old homes in
Waco, Texas a few years ago. Now they have a home
goods empire.

Most of the work is about making things new—
removing 80s wallpaper, opening floor plans, adding
marble kitchen islands. But without fail, homeowners
want something else. They want "character" in their
homes. Renovators go to great lengths to deliver.
They preserve turn-of-the-century woodwork, original Craftsman built-ins, authentic mid-century modern fireplaces. Or they import character. They install
old farmhouse beams in the ceiling; use a 1930s hutch
for a bookcase; a vintage front door instead of one
from Home Depot.

I'm not much for HGTV, but I find the interest in preserving character intriguing. Part of the draw is that stuff used to be better made. Woodwork from the early twentieth century still looks beautiful. Woodwork from the 90s belongs in a landfill. Ikea shelves are fine for the short term, but they look flimsy next to old built-ins. There's something else about it too. New things can be well made. But they don't yet have character. An old hutch has seen a few things. It's had a life. It tells a story, Joanna Gaines likes to say. On new items, nicks and scratches are defects. On a vintage piece they are ornaments. They are the marks of experience, of having lived a life.

In these final chapters, I draw attention to three marks of experience in the life of virtue: joy, wisdom, and peace. We might call them virtues, as some do. Or we might call them gifts, or perfections. Like virtues, cultivating them takes some attention, and at times, some effort. But in other ways they differ from the virtues. They seem less connected to action and more to a state of mind. They accompany the life of virtue rather than direct it. But the life of virtue would be incomplete without them. They are emblems of a mature moral life, the crowning jewels of virtue. Like marks on an old hutch, they reveal the victories and the struggles of life that, by God's grace, have been transformed from scratches and dents into ornaments of goodness.

WISDOM

WISDOM falls under the category of 'gifts of the Holy Spirit.' The Catechism of the Catholic Church explains that the gifts of the Holy Spirit "complete and perfect the virtues." It is the gift that builds upon and perfects knowledge. It does so with the help of faith. "The mind's understanding of eternal things leads to wisdom, rational understanding of temporal things only to knowledge," Augustine writes.[1] Wisdom points the mind heavenward. It also disposes us to see more in the ordinary things we know, by seeing their connection to God.

Emily Dickinson put it this way in her poem *'Nature' is what we see*. It reads:

---

1. Augustine, *De Trinitate*, 12.15

"Nature" is what we see—
The Hill—the Afternoon—
Squirrel—Eclipse—the Bumble bee—
Nay—Nature is Heaven—
Nature is what we hear—
The Bobolink—the Sea—
Thunder—the Cricket—
Nay—Nature is Harmony—
Nature is what we know—
Yet have no art to say—
So impotent Our Wisdom is
To her Simplicity.

Knowledge sees the obvious parts of reality—the hill, the afternoon, the squirrel. Wisdom sees that they are a reflection of Heaven, that the beauty we know has a deeper meaning. We know the sound of the cricket, thunder, the sea. Wisdom hears them as the harmony of God's creation. "For the spirit of the Lord fills the world, is all-embracing, and knows whatever is said," the book of Wisdom says. It is the wise person who seeks the Lord in all things.

Because of this, wisdom gives us a richer experience of life. The Jesuit theologian Hans Urs von

Balthasar liked to say that the truth is symphonic. "Glory be to God for dappled things," wrote another Jesuit. Both observed that God's goodness is expressed in the plurality of creation. Just as every instrument contributes its own sound to the orchestra, so every creature contributes its own goodness to the whole of creation. It is the task of wisdom to see and hear the unity in this plurality. The philosopher Blaise Pascal put it this way:[2]

It is the Gospel that brings contraries into accord through a skill entirely divine, and, uniting all that is true while banishing all that is false, makes the real wisdom of heaven where opposites, irreconcilable in human teaching, are harmonised.... This is the new and astonishing union that only God is able to teach ....

Pascal's words remind us that sometimes beauty, more than logic or philosophy, puts us in touch with wisdom. Pope Benedict XVI agreed. He once said that the most effective means of preaching the truth of Christianity is through the lives of its saints and the art that has been inspired by its faith.

2. Pascal, *Entretien avec M. de Saci*, OC 560.

Both of these things—art and the lives of the saints—instruct us through beauty. Both instruct us through suffering as well. The lives of the saints and martyrs are sometimes brutal examples of what happens when God's love touches a hostile world. The art of the Church often tries to capture their stories. More than that, it tries to uncover the beauty of a life lived for God. Both instruct us in wisdom. We learn from them that the disorder of this world will not be the last word. Divine love will. "Wisdom is by far the greatest part of joy," Sophocles writes in *Antigone*. The "mighty blows of fate" that cause us so much pain are also the means to that wisdom, and to joy.

But the suffering that brings us nearer to God, and therefore to wisdom, is not easy. That's the point. "Lord make me pure, but not yet," is everyone's favorite St. Augustine quote for a reason. It's natural to resist suffering, even when we know it will make us wise. That's why we have to ask for help. I began by saying that wisdom is a gift of the Holy Spirit. "Come Holy Ghost, creator blest ... Kindle our sense from above, And make our hearts o'erflow with love," the old hymn says. If we wish to be truly wise, we will have to ask him.

Let me close with three last pieces of advice. First, if you want to be wise, make time for contemplation. Wisdom puts eternal truth in touch with ordinary things. But ordinary, everyday things will always capture our attention if we let them. Carve out space in your life to set your mind on things above. It will change your perspective on everything.

Second, learn when to embrace suffering and when not to. Not all suffering leads to wisdom. The point is not to be a doormat, or to take abuse. Rather, it is to be undeterred in the desire to grow close to God, even when that comes at a price.

Finally, ask for grace. The path to wisdom requires help from others, and above all, from God. Don't make the mistake of trying to go it alone. Ask the Holy Spirit to be your guide.

PEACE

JESUS LISTS peacemaking among the beatitudes: "Blessed are the peacemakers, for they will be called children of God." All of us are God's children, so all of us are called to work for peace. Let me say two words about cultivating this virtue.

First, peace is more than the absence of conflict. St. Thomas observes that peace between one person and another requires that they share a desire for the same object, and that object must be something good for both of them. We don't achieve peace if one party consents to an agreement he thinks is unfair, because he has been forced or frightened. True peace, Aquinas says, requires charity. When we love other people as we love ourselves, we naturally desire the same thing as they do, because we want their good as much as we want our own.

As a lawyer I know that in that profession one learns to negotiate, arbitrate, mediate, to be a zealous advocate on behalf of clients. But the goal should never be to destroy a client's adversary or make him say "uncle." The aim should be a peaceful resolution to a case, which means a solution that is good for both parties. No one can make clients love their opponents. But we can show them how.

Second, as the Venerable Fulton Sheen once wrote, "There can be no world peace unless there is soul peace. [N]othing happens in the external world that has not first happened within a soul." If you want to bring peace to others, you need to cultivate it in your own heart. A Jesuit named Walter Ciszek entered the Soviet Union during the Second World War to quietly minister to Russian Catholics. Soon after, he was imprisoned, and later sentenced to fifteen years in labor camps. In a spiritual memoir he speaks of the crisis of faith that arose from his imprisonment. His year-long interrogation was filled with fear and anxiety. Hadn't he followed God's will? Where was the peace he was promised? Through prayer, Ciszek rediscovered something he already knew: peace is only found in total abandonment to God.

My life was to do the will of God ... His will would determine how long I would spend on earth .... My situation had not improved, but my disposition in the acceptance of God's will had returned. Along with it had come peace and a renewed confidence—not in my own ability to survive, but in a total trust and confidence in God's ability to sustain me and provide me with whatever strength I needed to meet the challenges he would send me. What greater peace and confidence could I require?

Few of us will face spiritual challenges as extreme as Ciszek's. His was a heroic peace. The challenges to our interior peace are more mundane. But the path to conquering them is the same. That's because the heart finds peace when it is at rest in the thing it really wants. "You have made us for yourself, O Lord, and our hearts are restless until they rest in you," says St. Augustine. The achievements of this world are good and worthy things, but they are not ends one can rest in. True peace is only found in God.

St. Francis de Sales offers this simple prescription for finding peace in your own heart: "Do all things for the glory of God.... Do the little that [you] can toward that end ... and leave it to God to take care of all the rest."

JOY

IT'S WORTH SPENDING some time thinking about joy, even though joy is not a virtue in the strict sense. The Church calls it a fruit of the Holy Spirit. Aquinas refers to it as an act, or effect, of the virtue of charity.

Joy is hard to pin down because it's often confused with other things, like pleasure. Zadie Smith, the British novelist, cautions against that confusion in a column in the *New York Review*. "A lot of people seem to feel that joy is only the most intense version of plea-sure, arrived at by the same road—you simply have to go a little further down the track," she writes. But joy and pleasure are different in a more fundamental sense. Joy is a more profound sentiment.

Profound, Smith says, but less agreeable. Joy has a downside that troubles her, an element of fear and sadness. A spouse or a child who brings us intense joy inevitably changes or dies, and leaves us behind. Smith says about joy what Julian Barnes once said about mourning: "It hurts just as much as it is worth." In the end she decides it is worth the trouble. If we never ex-perienced joy, she writes, "how would we live?"

This is true as far as it goes. And yet there is some-thing missing in Smith's account. She's right about joy and pleasure being different. But in her picture joy too is temporary. The house always wins, unless you have the good fortune to die while you're still holding good cards.

Smith's account is like Dorothy's view of Kansas before the tornado. Or like Harry Potter's life with the Dursleys. They are all unaware of a whole magi-cal world that exists side-by-side with their own and influences its activities. Smith leaves God out of the picture.

The psalmist tells us we find real joy in God's love: "The Lord has done great things for us," Psalm 126 says. "We are filled with joy." This is not the evanescent emotion Smith fears. Christian joy survives the death and change that make her experience of joy a zero-sum game. If we look carefully we will find an expression of God's love in everything we do: in the grace he gives us to do what is right; in the mercy he shows us when we fail.

That is the way to begin—by looking for God's love. But finding it is not a one-time thing. And enjoying it is like, in fact it is, being in love. We have to work at it. We have to find the joy in what comes our way. We have to learn to be joyful.

Flannery O'Connor had a pen pal named Betty Hester, who started by writing her fan mail and became a regular correspondent. They wrote back and forth every week. (This was before texting.) In one of her letters O'Connor writes to Hester about "what you call my struggle to submit." It is not, she says, a "struggle to submit but a struggle to accept and with passion. I mean, possibly, with joy. Picture me with my ground teeth stalking joy ...." I don't know about the teeth-grinding. But I agree about the struggle and the passion. Love is something we work at every day, and we give and accept it with passion. I mean, with joy.

Let me offer three pieces of advice for finding joy. First, don't be fooled by pleasure. Zadie Smith is right about that. It won't give you lasting joy, and it can distract you from the real thing. This is true about beer and sex and BMWs; fancy clothes, shiny phones, chic restaurants. Dana Gioia puts it perfectly in one of his poems (*Shopping*):

> *I would buy happiness if I could find it,*
> *Spend all that I possessed or could borrow.*
> *But what can I bring you from these sad emporia?*
> *Where in this splendid clutter*
> *Shall I discover the one true thing?*

Second, discover the thing in life that brings lasting satisfaction, and make that your priority. Loving God, your neighbor, your vocation—this will bring you joy in the long run. Ask yourself: will this matter to me in 10 years? 30 years? 50 years? If it won't, don't waste your time on it.

Finally, try to find God in all things. This is where Christian joy begins. It is sustained by loving him in all things. But that requires that you don't stop looking for him. Look for God. Love him. Be joyful.

WORKS CITED

À Kempis, Thomas. *Imitation of Christ*. Translated by William Benham. Project Gutenberg, https://www.gutenberg.org/ebooks/1653. Accessed on February 17, 2022.

Alighieri, Dante. *Inferno*. Translated by Robin Kirkpatrick. Penguin Classics, 2006.

Alighieri, Dante. *Paradiso*. Translated by Allen Mandelbaum. Digital Dante at Columbia University, https://digitaldante.columbia.edu/dante/divine-comedy/paradiso/paradiso-30/. Accessed on February 17, 2022.

Arias, Francis. *A Treatise of Benignity* (1630). Text Creation Partnership, https://quod.lib.umich.edu/e/eebo2/A21050.0001.001?view=toc. Accessed on February 17, 2022.

Aristotle, *Nicomachean Ethics*. Translated by D.P. Chase. Project Gutenberg, https://www.gutenberg.org/files/8438/8438-h/8438-h.htm. Accessed February 17, 2022.

Arnold, Matthew. "Growing Old." Poetry Foundation, https://www.poetryfoundation.org/poems/52311/growing-old. Accessed on February 17, 2022.

Arrupe, Pedro. "Men and Women for Others." Ignatian Solidarity, https://ignatiansolidarity.net/men-and-women-for-others-fr-pedro-arrupe-s-j/. Accessed February 16, 2022.

Augustine of Hippo. *City of God*. Translated by Marcus Dods. New Advent, https://www.newadvent.org/fathers/1201.htm. Accessed February 17, 2022.

Augustine of Hippo. *Confessions*. Translated by Henry Chadwick. Oxford World Classics, 2009.

Augustine of Hippo. *De Trinitate*. Translated by Arthur West

Haddan. New Advent, https://www.newadvent.org/fathers/1301.htm. Accessed February 17, 2022.

Austen, Jane. *Emma*. Wordsworth Classics, 1997.

Austen, Jane. *Northanger Abbey*. Wordsworth Classics, 1993.

Austen, Jane. *Mansfield Park*. Penguin Classics, 2003.

Austen, Jane. *Persuasion*. Everyman's Library, 1992.

Austen, Jane. *Pride and Prejudice*. Penguin Classics, 1996.

Austen, Jane. *Sense and Sensibility*. 3rd Edition. Oxford UP, 2019.

Benedict of Nursia. *Rule of St. Benedict*. Washbourne, 1875.

Benedict XVI. *Spe Salvi*. Vatican.va, https://www.vatican.va/content/benedict-xvi/en/encyclicals/documents/hf_ben-xvi_enc_20071130_spe-salvi.html. Accessed February 16, 2022.

Butler, Alban. *Butler's Lives of the Saints*. 2nd Ed. Christian Classics, 1956.

Catechism of the Catholic Church. Vatican.va, https://www.vatican.va/archive/ccc/index.htm. Accessed February 16, 2022.

Chambers, Whittaker. *Witness*. Regnery History, 2014.

Chesterton, G.K. *Orthodoxy*. Ignatius, 1995.

Ciszek, Walter. *He Leadeth Me*. Image, 1973.

Day, Dorothy. *The Reckless Way of Love*. Edited by Carolyn Kurtz. Plough, 2017.

De Sales, Francis. *Introduction to the Devout Life*. Veritatis Splendor, 2012.

Dickinson, Emily. "A Counterfeit—a Plated Person —." Dickinson Electronic Archives, http://archive.emilydickinson.org/working/hb157.htm. Accessed on February 17, 2022.

Dickinson, Emily. "Faith—is the Pierless Bridge." Amherst College Digital Collections, https://acdc.amherst.edu/view/asc:1322139. Accessed February 16, 2022.

Dickinson, Emily. "Hope is the Thing with Feathers." Poetry Foundation, https://www.poetryfoundation.org/poems/42889/hope-is-the-thing-with-feathers-314. Accessed February 16, 2022.

Dickinson, Emily. "My Worthiness is all my Doubt." Amherst College Digital Collections, https://acdc.amherst.edu/view/asc:1411704. Accessed on February 17, 2022.

Dickinson, Emily. "'Nature' is what we see—." Amherst College Digital Collections, https://acdc.amherst.edu/view/asc:1332806. Accessed February 17, 2022.

Dickinson, Emily. "'Remember me' implored the Thief!" Amherst College Digital Collections, https://acdc.amherst.edu/view/asc:1317781.

Dostoevsky, Fyodor. *The Brothers Karamazov*. Translated by Constance Garnett. The Macmillan Company, 1922.

Edmondson, Henry T. III. *A Political Companion to Flannery O'Connor*. University Press of Kentucky, 2017.

Escrivá, Josemaría. *Furrow*. Scepter, 1992.

Franklin, Benjamin. *The Autobiography of Benjamin Franklin*. Henry Holt and Company, 1916. Project Gutenberg, https://www.gutenberg.org/files/20203/20203-h/20203-h.htm. Accessed February 17, 2022.

Gaudium et Spes. Vatican.va, https://www.vatican.va/archive/hist_councils/ii_vatican_council/documents/vat-ii_const_19651207_gaudium-et-spes_en.html. Accessed February 17, 2022.

Gioia, Dana. "Shopping." *Pity the Beautiful*. Graywolf, 2012.

Greene, Graham. *Brighton Rock*. Penguin Classics, 2004.

Guardini, Romano. *Tree of Life*. Sophia Institute Press, 1987.

Hauerwas, Stanley. *The Hauerwas Reader*. Duke University Press, 2001.

Herbert, Anne. *Random Acts of Kindness and Senseless Acts of Beauty*. New Village, 2017.

Herbert, George. "Constancy." The George Herbert in Bemerton Group, https://www.georgeherbert.org.uk/archives/selected_work_37.html. Accessed February 17, 2022.

Hopkins, Gerard Manley. "Pied Beauty." Poetry Founda-

tion, https://www.poetryfoundation.org/poems/44399/
pied-beauty. Accessed on February 17, 2022.

Hughes, Langston. "Youth." Poets.org, https://poets.org/poem/
youth-0. Accessed on February 17, 2020.

Hugo, Victor. *Les Misérables.* Translated by Isabel F. Hapgood.
Thomas Y. Cowell & Co., 1887.

John of the Cross. *The Collected Works of St. John of the Cross.*
Translated by Kavanaugh and Rodriguez. ICS Publications,
1991.

John Paul II. *Dilecti Amici.* Vatican.va, https://www.vatican.va/
content/john-paul-ii/en/apost_letters/1985/documents/
hf_jp-ii_apl_31031985_dilecti-amici.html. Accessed on
February 17, 2020.

John Paul II. *Fides et Ratio.* Vatican.va, https://www.vatican
.va/content/john-paul-ii/en/encyclicals/documents/hf_
jp-ii_enc_14091998_fides-et-ratio.html. Accessed February
16, 2022.

King, Martin Luther, Jr.. "Nonviolence and Racial Justice." *Christian Century,* 6 February 1957, https://kinginstitute.stanford.
edu/king-papers/documents/nonviolence-and-racial-justice.
Accessed February 16, 2022.

Lewis, C.S. *The Complete C.S. Lewis Signature Classics.* Harper-
Collins, 2002.

Lincoln, Abraham. *Abraham Lincoln: His Speeches and Writings.*
Edited by Roy P. Basler. Da Capo, 1946.

MacIntyre, Alasdair. *After Virtue.* Notre Dame, 1984.

Mattison, William C., III. *Introducing Moral Theology: True
Happiness and the Virtues.* Brazos, 2008.

May, William F. "The Virtues and Vices of the Elderly." *What
Does it Mean to Grow Old?: Reflections from the Humanities.*
eds. Cole, T.R. and Gadow, S.. Duke, 1950.

O'Connor, Flannery. *Letters to Betty Hester.* Emory University, Stuart A. Rose Manuscript, Archives, and Rare Book
Library.

WORKS CITED

Oliver, Mary. *Upstream: Selected Essays*. Penguin Books, 2019.

Pascal, Blaise. *Entretien avec M. de Saci*. Quoted in *In the Light of Christ* by Lucy Beckett. Ignatius, 2006.

Pieper, Joseph. *The Four Cardinal Virtues*. Notre Dame, 1990.

Plato. *Republic*. Translated by Benjamin Jowett. Project Gutenberg, https://www.gutenberg.org/files/1497/1497-h/1497-h.htm. Accessed February 17, 2022.

Pope, Alexander. "The Universal Prayer." Poetry Foundation, https://www.poetryfoundation.org/poems/50590/the-universal-prayer. Accessed February 16, 2022.

Pope Francis. "Homily for the Holy Mass for the Opening of the Synod of Bishops for the Pan-Amazon Region." Vatican.va, https://www.vatican.va/content/francesco/en/homilies/2019/documents/papa-francesco_20191006_omelia-sinodo-amazzonia.html. Accessed February 17, 2022.

Putnam, Robert. *Bowling Alone*. Simon & Schuster, 2000.

Rossetti, Christina. "A Pause of Thought." *Delphi Poet Series: Christina Rossetti*. Delphi Classics, 2012.

Shakespeare, William. *Julius Caesar. William Shakespeare: The Complete Works*. 2nd ed., edited by Stanley Wells and Gary Taylor. Clarendon, 2005.

Shakespeare, William. *The Merchant of Venice. William Shakespeare: The Complete Works*. 2nd Ed., edited by Stanley Wells and Gary Taylor. Clarendon, 2005.

Shakespeare, William. *The Tragedy of Othello. William Shakespeare: The Complete Works*. 2nd Ed., edited by Stanley Wells and Gary Taylor. Clarendon, 2005.

Sheen, Fulton. *Go to Heaven*. Ignatius, 2017.

Sheen, Fulton. *Peace of Soul*. Liguori, 1996.

Sheen, Fulton. *The Seven Virtues*. Garden City Books, 1953.

Smith, Zadie. "Joy." The New York Review, https://www.nybooks.com/articles/2013/01/10/joy/. Accessed on February 17, 2020.

WORKS CITED

Supreme Court of the United States. *Planned Parenthood of Southeastern Pennsylvania v. Robert P. Casey.* Nos. 91–744, 91–902, 29 June 1992, Cornell Law School Legal Information Institute, https://www.law.cornell.edu/supremecourt/text/505/833.

Thérèse of Lisieux. *The Story of a Soul.* 3rd ed. ICS Publications, 1996.

Tolkien, J.R.R.. *The Fellowship of the Ring.* William Morrow Paperbacks, 2012.

Waugh, Evelyn. *Brideshead Revisited.* Back Bay Books, 1973.

Weil, Simone. *Waiting for God.* Harper Perennial Modern Classics, 2009.

Wordsworth, William. "Nuns Fret Not at Their Convent's Narrow Room." Poetry Foundation, https://www.poetryfoundation.org/poems/52299/nuns-fret-not-at-their-convents-narrow-room. Accessed February 16, 2022.

The Virtues was designed in Dante and
composed by Kachergis Book Design
of Pittsboro, North Carolina. It was
printed on 55# Rolland Enviro Natural
and bound by Freisens of Altona,
Canada.